To Vince,

for a better

life and understanding.

Merry Christmas!

Zita

THE DOCTRINE AND COVENANTS

OUR MODERN SCRIPTURE

THE DOCTRINE AND COVENANTS

OUR MODERN SCRIPTURE

Revised and Enlarged

Richard O. Cowan

Bookcraft
Salt Lake City, Utah

Library of Congress Catalog Card Number: 84-72192
ISBN 0-88494-545-6

First Bookcraft Edition

First Printing, 1984
2nd Printing, 1985

Lithographed in the United States of America

Contents

Sources Frequently Cited

CR: *Conference Reports* of The Church of Jesus Christ of Latter-day Saints.

D&C Commentary: Hyrum M. Smith and Janne M. Sjodahl, *The Doctrine and Covenants Commentary* (Salt Lake City: Deseret Book Co., 1955).

HC: Joseph Smith, *History of The Church of Jesus Christ of Latter-day Saints*, ed. B. H. Roberts, 7 vols. (Salt Lake City: The Church of Jesus Christ of Latter-day Saints, 1932-51).

JD: *Journal of Discourses*, 26 vols. (London: Latter-day Saints Book Depot, 1855-86).

Sperry, *Compendium*: Sidney B. Sperry, *Doctrine and Covenants Compendium* (Salt Lake City: Bookcraft, 1960).

Teachings: Joseph Smith, *Teachings of the Prophet Joseph Smith*, ed. Joseph Fielding Smith (Salt Lake City: Deseret Book Co., 1938).

List of Illustrations

Photographs and Engravings

Maps

Charts

Preface

For more than seventeen years I have had the privilege of teaching classes in the Doctrine and Covenants at Brigham Young University. Each year I have become increasingly impressed with the profound doctrinal teachings and the significant ecclesiastical instructions contained in this volume of modern scripture. While helping to write the Sunday School Gospel Doctrine lessons for 1978–80 dealing with the Doctrine and Covenants and with subsequent Church history, I recognized anew the vital importance of continuous revelation through living prophets.

Now it is my desire to share this testimony as well as insights which have proved helpful in my classes on campus. Therefore, this book includes explanations, charts, and other materials which should assist your study of the Doctrine and Covenants. It has not been my purpose here to discuss every point at length. You will, therefore, wish to enrich your learning by consulting commentaries or other works on the Doctrine and Covenants; for this purpose a brief bibliography and some specific references have been included herein.

The material in this book has been arranged chronologically, considering the various sections in sequence as they appear in the Doctrine and Covenants. Numerous cross-references will help you locate pertinent information elsewhere in the book.

This study guide will help to set the revelations in the Doctrine and Covenants in the context of United States history as well as Church developments. In addition to considerations of basic Doctrine and Covenants teachings, there are brief comments which may help you better understand specific passages. It is hoped that the deliberate brevity of this work will encourage you to study the scriptures themselves.

It is my firm conviction and testimony that the Doctrine and Covenants is the word of the Lord given in this dispensation through a living prophet.

Introduction

Modern Revelation and the Doctrine and Covenants

Perhaps the most basic difference between The Church of Jesus Christ of Latter-day Saints and all other churches in the world is its claim to continuous modern revelation. In a world beset with so many problems and where there are so many conflicting opinions about religion, teachings of a living prophet who is authorized to declare the word of God are of the greatest importance in knowing the truth. Of the four books which Latter-day Saints accept as scripture, the Doctrine and Covenants is truly the most modern because it contains teachings which not only apply to our day, but which have been given in our day. (See Roy W. Doxey, *The Doctrine and Covenants Speaks*, chap. 1.)

Biblical Teachings on Continuous Revelation

An ancient biblical proverb declared, "Where there is no vision, the people perish." (Proverbs 29:18.) The prophet Amos also testified, "Surely the Lord God will do nothing, but he revealeth his secret unto his servants the prophets." (Amos 3:7.) Furthermore, the Bible itself sets forth the example of continuous revelation through divinely appointed prophets.

Through the prophet Nephi, the Lord promised continued revelation, "that I may prove ... that I am the same yesterday, today, and forever." He then added, "And because that I have spoken one word ye need not suppose that I cannot speak another; for my work is not yet finished; neither shall it be until the end of man, neither from that time henceforth and forever." (2 Nephi 29:9; compare Hebrews 13:8.)

The Bible specifically predicts latter-day revelation which would come through Elijah (Malachi 4:5-6), Elias (Matthew 17:11), an angel (Revelation 14:6-7), and even through Christ himself (Acts 3:19-21). Thus, "in the dispensation of the fulness of times he [the Lord] might gather together in one all things in Christ, both which are in heaven and which are on earth." (Ephesians 1:10.)

Some people have objected to modern revelation because of two biblical statements:

1. The apostle Paul told Timothy that "the holy scriptures . . . are able to make thee wise unto salvation." (2 Timothy 3:15.) If the scriptures were sufficient for salvation in Paul's day, these critics assert, there is no need for any additional scriptures. One must remember, however, that the "holy scriptures" of Paul's time would not have included the New Testament books (such as Paul's very epistle to Timothy), which were canonized only centuries later.

2. At the end of his Revelation, John warned, "I testify unto every man that heareth the words of the prophecy of this book, If any man shall add unto these things, God shall add unto him the plagues that are written in this book." (Revelation 22:18.) Opponents to latter-day revelation argue that John was forbidding additions to the biblical scripture. The Bible as a whole, as already noted, was not yet gathered together and canonized; in fact, many scholars believe that John wrote his Gospel and Epistles after recording the Revelation. Thus the phrase "this book" in his warning must have referred only to the book of Revelation itself. Ancient authors often included such warnings against tampering with their texts; note similar declarations in the book of Deuteronomy (4:2; 12:32). Furthermore, John prohibited only human and not divine additions to his prophecy. Finally, the Bible refers to several scriptural books not found in today's biblical canon. (See the list of "Missing Scriptures" in James E. Talmage, *The Articles of Faith*, Appendix 13:8.) For example, as John concluded his Gospel he acknowledged that there were still many of the Savior's deeds left unrecorded (John 21:25;) surely we ought to accept these and any others of his words which might be revealed to us.

How Revelations Come

There are several means by which revelation, or communication from God, may come. These may be considered under the following headings:

1. Personal visitations—such as by Moroni (sec. 2), John the Baptist (sec. 13), an angel (sec. 27), the Savior, Moses, Elias, and Elijah (sec. 110).

2. Visions—such as section 76 on the three degrees of glory. Objects or persons may be seen or heard as though they were physically present even though they are not.

3. Revelation through mechanical devices—such as the Urim and Thummim, Liahona, etc. Note that half of the revelations given through Joseph Smith before he received the Melchizedek Priesthood (sections 3, 6, 7, 11, 14, 15, 16, and 17) came through the Urim and Thummim.

4. Inspiration—or revelation by direct action of the Spirit upon the recipient's mind. Ideas received from the Lord must be then expressed by men "after the manner of their language." (D&C 1:24.)

5. In "spiritual confirmation" the individual takes the initiative by first studying a matter out in his own mind and then asking God "if it be right." (D&C 9:7-9.) Thus, contrary to the popular notion, dramatic revelation such as personal visits and visions figured rarely in receiving the revelations now in the Doctrine and Covenants; rather, inspiration and spiritual confirmation, the channels through which most individuals receive answers to their personal prayers, were also the means most often used in giving these recorded revelations. (See William E. Berrett, *Teachings of the Doctrine and Covenants*, chap. 3.)

The Doctrine and Covenants

"Doctrines" are the basic saving truths of the gospel of Jesus Christ. "Covenants" are solemn agreements in which the Lord promises mighty blessings to those who keep their commitments to him. An earlier title identified the compiled revelation as "The Book of Commandments." The Lord himself described this volume as a "voice of warning." A profitable approach to studying this book might involve identifying these great doctrines, covenants, commandments, and warnings, and pondering their relevance to our lives today.

Composition of the Book

The title page of the Doctrine and Covenants indicates that this volume contains "Revelations Given to Joseph Smith, the Prophet, With some Additions by his Successors in the Presidency of the Church." Although 128 of the 136 sections in the Doctrine and Covenants can be classified as direct revelations, others are of a different nature. Section 102, for example, is an extract from the minutes of a meeting; sections 123, 127, and 128 are letters, sections 130 and 131 are items of instruction given by Joseph Smith; and sections 134 and 135 are official statements drawn up by Church leaders. Even though these sections may not be *direct* revelations in the sense that they actually quote words spoken by the Lord, still they are *indirect* revelation and should be regarded as "the word of the Lord" because they include previously revealed truths.

Note that the New Testament is composed of historical accounts—the four Gospels and the book of Acts—as well as letters written by Paul and others. The Old Testament, Book of Mormon, and Pearl of Great Price follow a similar pattern. Thus, of the four standard works, the Doctrine and Covenants actually has the highest proportion of material that may be classified as direct revelation. Furthermore, the entire book is scripture (1) because it contains teachings written or spoken by those in authority as they have been "moved upon by the Holy Ghost" (D&C 68:2-4), and (2) because the book has been accepted by the Church as canonized scripture (at the general conference, Oct. 10, 1880).

Coming Forth

The First Vision or appearance of the Father and the Son to Joseph Smith during the early spring of 1820 was the first communication from God through a living prophet in our time and, thus, opened the present dispensation. Even though this revelation is not included in the Doctrine and Covenants, it should still be studied for the important truths which became the foundation for subsequent revelations. Read Joseph Smith's history of this experience in the Pearl of Great Price. (Joseph Smith 2:5-20.)

Other revelations followed, restoring basic gospel principles necessary for reestablishing God's kingdom on earth. The first of these, Moroni's visit of September 21, 1823, is now recorded as section 2.

The Church of Jesus Christ was formally organized on April 6, 1830. At its first regular conference, held in Fayette, New York, on June 9, 1830, the "Articles and Covenants [were] read by Joseph Smith, Jr., and received by unanimous vote of the whole conference." (Minutes taken by Oliver Cowdery, quoted in *Far West Record*, p. 1.) The "Articles and Covenants" consisted of the revelations now known as sections 20 and 22. This document was reviewed at most of the Church's early conferences and can well be regarded as the forerunner of our modern book of scripture, the Doctrine and Covenants. During this same year, 1830, Joseph Smith began the work of collecting, copying, and arranging the revelations in preparation for possible publication. (*HC*, 1:104.)

The special conference held November 1, 1831, decided to publish 10,000 copies of the Book of Commandments, although the number was reduced to 3,000 the following year. This edition contained 65 chapters and was similar in content and arrangement to the first 64 sections in the present Doctrine and Covenants. In 1833 a mob destroyed the plant in which the Book of Commandments was being printed, not so much because of displeasure with the publication of the compiled revelations but because of opposition to a Latter-day Saint newspaper, the *Evening and Morning Star,* which was being issued from the same press. Nevertheless, the result was that only a few copies of the partially completed book remained.

During the fall of 1834 a committee composed of members of the First Presidency was constituted to bring the compilation of revelations up to date and publish it in book form. The 1835 edition appeared under the title of Doctrine and Covenants. Its first part was entitled "Theology" and included the "Lectures on Faith." (See the discussion of these lectures below.) The second part, entitled "Covenants and Commandments of the Lord," included the revelations. Thus the book's new title reflected these two divisions. This compilation included 102 sections which covered about the same material as the first 107 sections plus sections 133 and 134 in the present Doctrine and Covenants. The former chronological order was abandoned in favor of an arrangement which grouped the more significant revelations near the beginning of the book. At the conference where this book was officially accepted as scripture, the Twelve Apostles (a quorum which had just recently been brought into being) signed a testimony almost identical to that which the witnesses to the Book of Commandments had set forth four years earlier.

Because of the quantity printed in 1835, the next major edition of the Doctrine and Covenants was not issued until 1844, just a short time following the Prophet's martyrdom. It included 111 sections and was similar in arrangement to the 1835 edition.

The 1876 edition, prepared under the supervision of Orson Pratt of the Council of the Twelve, returned to the basic chronological arrangement and included the same 136 sections in the same order as in the current edition. Twenty-four revelations given through Joseph Smith, as well as the 1847 revelation to Brigham Young, were included for the first time. For the first time, the sections were divided into verses, and historical notes and footnote references were included.

In the present or 1921 edition, which was prepared under the direction of Elder James E. Talmage of the Quorum of the Twelve, the historical notes and cross-references were improved and the text was printed in double columns. The "Lectures on Faith" which had been included in several previous editions were omitted. (For a chart summarizing the key editions of the Doctrine and Covenants, see Appendix A.)

Chronological Order of Contents

The list of the revelations summarized in Chart 1 reflects the geographical progression of Church history. The fact that many revelations were necessary to restore the fundamental truths at and immediately following the organization of the Church explains why more recorded revelations were received during 1830 and 1831 than during any other similar period.

Chart 1

Geographical and Chronological Distribution
of Doctrine and Covenants Sections

Place	1823–1828	1829	1830	1831	1832	1833	1834–1837	1838	1839–1844	1847	Total
Manchester, N.Y.	1		3								4
Harmony, Pa.	2	9	4								15
Fayette, N.Y.		5	12	3							20
Kirtland, Ohio				19	5	12	10				46
Hiram, Ohio				7	8						15
Misc.—Ohio				2	1						3
Jackson Co., Mo.				4	2						6
Far West, Mo.								7			7
Misc.—Mo.				2			1	1	3		7
Nauvoo, Ill.*									10		10
Others						1	1			1	3
Totals	3	14	19	37	16	13	12	8	13	1	136

*Vicinity

What to Look For in Each Section

Having the following information about each revelation will
help increase one's appreciation of the Doctrine and Covenants:

1. What circumstances, questions, problems, etc., brought forth
the revelation? How does the general historical setting give
meaning to specific points in the revelation?

2. How did the Lord deal with these circumstances, answer
the questions, solve the problems, etc.?

3. How did this revelation influence an individual's later life
or subsequent Church history?

4. What are the important teachings in the section? These of-

Areas Related to the Doctrine and Covenants

ten go far beyond the circumstances which brought forth the revelation.

5. What ideas in the section are especially inspiring to you personally? Even though these revelations were given in specific settings to designated persons, they still contain principles which are as applicable today as ever.

The "Lectures on Faith"

A series of seven lectures was written for use in the School of the Prophets during the winter of 1834-35. They were printed with the Doctrine and Covenants but were never regarded as being equal in value to the revelations contained in that volume. Note the distinction made by the Kirtland high council in its testimony about the Doctrine and Covenants. Representing the council, John Smith wrote that "the revelations in said book were true, and that the lectures were judiciously written and compiled and were profitable for doctrine." (*HC*, 2:176.) Even though they were edited by the Prophet Joseph Smith, "they were never presented to nor accepted by the Church as being otherwise than theological lectures or lessons." Therefore, they were omitted from the 1921 edition of the Doctrine and Covenants. Since then they have been published in pamphlet form with comments by Elder John A. Widtsoe of the Council of the Twelve.

The lectures point out that faith is the first principle of religion and the foundation of righteousness. Faith is a principle of power—the power by which God created and now governs the universe. In order for faith in God to be a real source of power, the individual must—

1. know that God exists, a fact upheld by the testimonies of the prophets right from the time of Adam;

2. have a correct idea of God's character, attributes, and perfections;

3. know that the course of one's own life is in agreement with God's will. One must be willing to sacrifice all that he has in order to obtain this assurance.

The "Lectures on Faith" point out that the fruits which grow from such faith include all of the blessings of eternity which God has in store for his children.

Sections 1 – 138

Section 1: The Lord's Preface

Even though this revelation was recorded between sections 66 and 67, it has been placed first because it is intended to be the Lord's preface to the book of his commandments which was about to be published. (See the discussion of section 67 for a more detailed account of the setting for section 1.)

A "Voice of Warning" (Verses 1–16). It is customary for the author of a book to give in the preface his reasons for writing the work and a brief prospectus of its message. In this preface, the Lord, who is the true Author of the Doctrine and Covenants, described his message as a "voice of warning" which should go "unto all people." (verse 4.)

The Lord likened today's world to the ancient materialistic and wicked kingdoms of Babylon and Idumea. (Verses 16 and 36.) In another revelation he characterized "wickedness" as "spiritual Babylon." (See D&C 133:14.) Idumea was the kingdom of the Edomites, who were descendants of Esau. This people frequently was the object of warnings sounded by the Lord's prophets. (See, for example, Isaiah 34:5, Ezekiel 36:5, and the book of Obadiah.) Similarly, the Lord knows that unless the wicked in our day repent, calamities must certainly come upon them. Because of his love for his children on earth, he therefore gave these commandments as a warning: "Prepare ye, prepare ye for that which is to come, for the Lord is nigh." (verse 12.)

Fruits of the Lord's Revelations (Verses 17–30). Because the Lord has spoken from heaven, the weak (at least in the eyes of the world) will be able to confound the proud. (Compare verses 17–19 with

1 Corinthians 1:27.) Furthermore, his servants need *not* counsel with human wisdom alone, but rather may "speak in the name of God the Lord." (Compare verses 19–20 with 2 Nephi 28:31.) In verses 21–28 the Lord outlined other results of his having restored the gospel by means of the revelations contained in the Doctrine and Covenants. Ponder how the same consequences might similarly affect the lives of all who study this book today.

The Lord Speaks in Our Language (Verse 24). In order to communicate more perfectly, the Lord is willing to address his children "in their weakness, after the manner of their language." (Verse 24.) While language is an important medium of communication, it can also become a limitation. If the precisely right word cannot be found, it is more difficult to communicate the desired meaning accurately. For example, the ancient prophet Mormon lamented that "there are many things which, according to our language, we are not able to write." (3 Nephi 5:18.) His son Moroni explained that to conserve space the Nephites wrote in "reformed Egyptian," and that "if we could have written in Hebrew" there would have been "no imperfection in our record." Nevertheless, he explained, the Lord "prepared means" for us to overcome these difficulties and to obtain a proper interpretation. (Mormon 9:32–34.) Similarly, if we read the revelations in the Doctrine and Covenants with the Lord's Spirit, he can reveal his message anew directly to us, thus bypassing any barriers to complete understanding which may be posed by Joseph Smith's nineteenth-century language.

One True Church (Verses 30–33). Because the Restored Church asserts a unique claim to divine authority by direct revelation, it has never considered participating in mergers with other churches as part of the ecumenical movement. This does not mean that some good may not be found in any other organization. Furthermore, verse 30 points out that mere membership in the "true Church" does not necessarily guarantee an individual's righteousness. Humility rather than boastfulness, therefore, is the proper attitude for a Latter-day Saint.

In verses 30–33 the Lord explained that he could not tolerate sin even among his "only true and living church." (For a more complete discussion of the relationship between repentance and forgiveness, see the discussion under section 19.)

The Place of the Living Prophet (Verse 38). On the very day the Church was organized, the Lord commanded the Latter-day Saints to receive the Prophet's words "as if from mine own mouth." (D&C 21:4-5.) In his preface to the Doctrine and Covenants, the Lord bore witness of his earthly representatives' authority: "What I the Lord have spoken, I have spoken, and I excuse not myself; and though the heavens and earth pass away, my word shall not pass away, but shall all be fulfilled, whether by mine own voice, or by the voice of my servants, it is the same." (D&C 1:38.)

Thus in addition to the written scripture from the past, Latter-day Saints are blessed with "living scripture" in the present. Elder Henry D. Moyle, a counselor in the First Presidency, observed:

"The older I get and the closer the contact I have with the President of the Church, the more I realize that the greatest of all scriptures which we have in the world today is current scripture.... And I love it more than all other. It applies to me today specifically, and to you all." (BYU Fireside Address, January 1963.)

Elder Marion G. Romney has testified, "What the Presidency say as a Presidency is what the Lord would say if he were here, and it is scripture. It should be studied, understood, and followed, even as the revelations in the Doctrine and Covenants." (*CR,* April 1945, pp. 88-90.)

At the conclusion of a general conference, Elder Harold B. Lee admonished Church members to "consider seriously the importance of taking with them the report of this conference and let it be the guide to their walk and talk during the next six months. These are the important matters the Lord sees fit to reveal to this people in this day." (*CR,* April 1946, p. 68.) In the same spirit Elder Spencer W. Kimball counseled us to obtain our own copy of the most recent conference talks (such as published in *the Ensign*): "Underline the pertinent thoughts and keep it with you for continual reference. No text or volume outside of the standard works of the Church should have a more prominent place on your personal library shelves." (BYU Devotional Address, May 14, 1968.)

Let us be eager to receive and live according to this most modern of all scripture. (For a discussion of revelations since the compilation of the Doctrine and Covenants, see p. 211.)

Section 2

About three and a half years following the appearance of the Father and the Son, Joseph Smith received his next heavenly communication. During the night of Sunday, September 21, and morning of Monday, September 22, 1823, the angel Moroni visited him three times and told him about a set of ancient sacred records from which the Book of Mormon was subsequently translated. Section 2 includes only a small extract from Moroni's message. Read the more complete account in Joseph Smith's history as found in the Pearl of Great Price. (verses 38–47.) In order to stress the urgency of the translation and publication of the Book of Mormon, Moroni cited several Old Testament prophecies concerning the last days and indicated that they were about to be fulfilled. Notice how the selection from Malachi's prophecy (as also found in section 2) supported this total message. In his Wentworth Letter account of these events, Joseph Smith quoted Moroni as emphasizing that "the preparatory work for the second coming was speedily to commence; that the time was at hand for the gospel in all its fulness to be preached in power, unto all nations that a people might be prepared for the Millennial reign." (*HC,* 4:537.)

Moroni's Revision of Malachi's Prophecy. Compare Moroni's version as given in section 2 with the corresponding passage in the King James Bible, Malachi 4:5–6.

Doctrine and Covenants Section 2	King James Bible Malachi 4:5–6
1. Behold, I will reveal unto you the Priesthood, by the hand of Elijah the prophet,	5. Behold, I will send you Elijah the prophet
before the coming of the great and dreadful day of the Lord.	before the coming of the great and dreadful day of the Lord.

2. And he shall plant in the hearts of the children the promises made to the fathers,

and the hearts of the children shall turn to their fathers.

3. If it were not so, the whole earth would be utterly wasted at his coming.

6. And he shall turn the heart of the fathers to the children,

and the hearts of the children to their fathers,

lest I come and smite the earth with a curse.

This same prophecy appears in the Book of Mormon (3 Nephi 25:5–6) and in Joseph Smith's inspired revision of the Bible, identically as it is found in the King James Version. This suggests that the Bible version must be correct, and, therefore, that Moroni's changes were more in the nature of revision for clarification and emphasis rather than being corrections of erroneous translations.

Priesthood to Be Revealed (Verse 1). The priesthood which Elijah restored in 1836 included the "sealing keys" by which not only the work for the dead, but all ordinances, may be performed on earth so that they will be sealed or "bound in heaven." (See Matthew 16:19; for a further consideration of Elijah's mission, see the discussion under section 110 herein.) The "great and dreadful day" refers to judgments which will accompany Christ's second coming.

Promises to the Fathers (Verse 2). "Fathers" may refer to those who died without an opportunity to accept and live the gospel of Jesus Christ. Many of them accepted the gospel when it was preached to them in the spirit world. (See 1 Peter 3:18–20; 4:6.)

President Joseph F. Smith explained the meaning of "the promises made to the fathers" by pointing out that "those who died without opportunity to receive ordinances necessary for exaltation were promised that the children in the last days would perform them in their behalf." (*CR,* October 1897, p. 47.) To explain why certain individuals receive the gospel and others do not, Elder Melvin J. Ballard testified, "It was made known to me that it is because of the righteous dead who had received the Gospel in the spirit world exercising themselves, and in answer to their prayers Elders of the Church were sent to the homes of their posterity that the Gospel might be taught to them and through their righteousness they might be privileged to have a descendant in the flesh do the work for their dead kindred.... It is with greater intensity that the hearts of the fathers and mothers in the spirit world are turned to their children than that our hearts are turned to them." (*Three Degrees of Glory,* p. 27.)

Elder Harold B. Lee added a new dimension to our understanding of Malachi's prophecy. He explained that one objective of Church programs, such as family home evening, is "to turn here upon the earth, the hearts of parents to children and the hearts of the children to parents. Can you believe that when parents have passed beyond the veil that then is the only time when parents should have their hearts turned to their children and children to their parents? ... Maybe it is time for us to think of turning the hearts of parents to children now while living in order that, after they are gone to the beyond, there might be that bond between parents and children that might last beyond death." ("Preparing to Meet the Lord," an address given by Elder Harold B. Lee at the dedication of the Oakland Temple in November 1964, *Improvement Era,* February 1965, p. 124.)

Section 3 and the Lost Manuscript

Joseph received the Book of Mormon records from Moroni on September 22, 1827. By April 1828, the Prophet had started the work of translation with the help of Martin Harris as scribe in Harmony, Pennsylvania.

By the month of June, 116 pages of manuscript had been written. Joseph recorded that—

Sometime after Mr. Harris had begun to write for me, he began to importune me to give him liberty to carry the writings home [to Palmyra, New York] and show them; and desired of me that I would inquire of the Lord through the Urim and Thummim, if he might not do so. I did inquire, and the answer was that he must not. However, he was not satisfied with this answer, and desired that I should inquire again. I did so, and the answer was as before. Still he could not be contented, but insisted that I should inquire once more. After much solicitation I again inquired of the Lord, and permission was granted him to have the writings on certain conditions. (HC, 1:21.)

Martin Harris failed to adhere strictly to these conditions, and through his carelessness the manuscript was lost. Because Martin did not return when expected, Joseph Smith himself went to Palmyra to learn what had happened. Shortly after his return to Harmony, a heavenly messenger appeared and returned the Urim and Thummim which had been taken from the Prophet because of his "having wearied the Lord in asking for permission of letting Martin Harris take the writings." (*HC*, 1:22.) This is the setting in which section 3 was received. The Urim and Thummim, as well as the Book of Mormon plates, were then again taken away, but both were returned a few days later when the Lord gave Joseph Smith some instructions (Section 10) about continuing the work of translation. (See *HC*, 1:21–23.) The Lord rebuked Joseph Smith and Martin Harris in these revelations and even referred to them as being "wicked" because they had placed their own judgment ahead of the Lord's counsel. The presence of such revelations in the Doctrine and Covenants should strengthen one's testimony that Joseph Smith truly was a prophet, because he would not likely have included them unless he knew they were revelations from God.

The Book of Mormon and the Lamanites (Verses 16–20). Even though the Book of Mormon was written for the "convincing of the Jew and Gentile that JESUS is the CHRIST," Doctrine and Covenants 3:20 suggests that this work shall have particular value for the Lamanites. This is in agreement with numerous Book of Mormon passages (such as Moroni 10:1–5) which indicate that the book was being written for the benefit of the latter-day Lamanites.

Who Are the Lamanites Today? In contrast to the idea that all the descendants of Nephi were killed in the last great battle at Cumorah, verses 17 and 18 in section 3 suggests that the so-called Lamanites may include descendants from Nephi and others as well. For about five hundred years the Nephites and Lamanites continued as two separate groups—the righteous prophets who kept the Book of Mormon record being among the Nephites, the Lamanites generally being

Chart 2

Who Are the Lamanites?

600 B.C.

Falling away of Laman
and Lemuel. They are
cursed. (2 Nephi 5:20-
23.)

*Lamanite
blood line*

Lamanites

Large number of La-
manite converts. People
of Ammon. (Alma 23:5;
24:29.)

More than half of
Lamanites converted.
(Helaman 6:1-2.)

Righteous Lamanites
adopted name "Ne-
phites." (3 Nephi
2:11-16.)

A.D. 1

Rebellious adopted the
name "Lamanites."
(4 Nephi 20.)

A.D. 400

Only the people called
"Lamanites" remained after
Moroni's death.

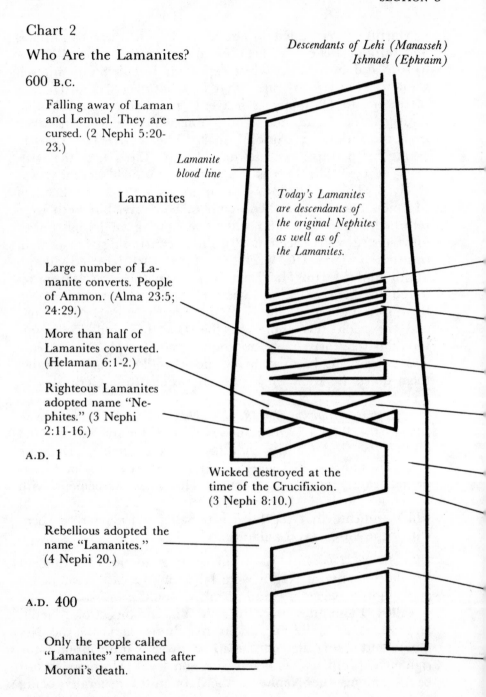

*Descendants of Lehi (Manasseh)
Ishmael (Ephraim)*

*Today's Lamanites
are descendants of
the original Nephites
as well as of
the Lamanites.*

Wicked destroyed at the
time of the Crucifixion.
(3 Nephi 8:10.)

Nephite
blood line

Nephites

Some Nephites remained
behind when Mosiah led
the righteous to Zara-
helma. (Omni 12, 13.)

Amulon led the wicked
priests of Noah. (Mosiah
20:1-5; 23:32-39.)

Apostate followers of
Nehor and Amlicites.
(Alma 1 and 2.)

Apostate Zoramites.
(Alma 31-35.)

More than half of Ne-
phites joined Lamanites.
(Helaman 6:2; 7-8, 21.)

Wicked Nephites and
Lamanites combined as
Gadianton Robbers.
(Helaman 11:24-33.)

People completely righteous
and united as a result
of the crucifixion and
Jesus' visit. (4 Nephi 17.)

Nephite dissenters flee
to Lamanites (Moroni 9:24.)

Nephite nation de-
stroyed in battle at
Cumorah. (Mormon 6.)   Compiled by Richard and Dawn Cowan

characterized as a wild, wicked, and warlike people. From 91 to 77 B.C., the four sons of Mosiah were the first who preached the gospel effectively among the Lamanites. As a result, many were converted, left their homeland, and were absorbed into the Nephite nation. In the meantime, groups of apostate Nephites were similarly assimilated among the Lamanites. Another very successful mission in about 30 B.C. brought such widespread conversion among both Nephites and Lamanites that, in effect, both groups became one people for a time. Just before the coming of Christ, a reversal of the traditional role was evident when Samuel, a Lamanite prophet, was sent to call the Nephites to repentance.

Following the visit of the resurrected Savior, righteousness prevailed for about two hundred years, during which period there were no divisions among the people. In A.D. 231, a new dividing line was drawn—the unbelievers adopted the name Lamanites, while the faithful called themselves Nephites. Each group consisted of several subdivisions. (Read 4 Nephi 35–39.) Thus, the Lamanites included descendants not only of Laman but also of Nephi.

Over a century later, the majority of the Nephites had become so wicked that the Lord permitted the less wicked Lamanites to destroy them in the battle of Cumorah in about A.D. 385. During this final battle, many Nephites defected to the Lamanites. This may explain the meaning of Doctrine and Covenants 3:17–18 (compare 4 Nephi 35–39) and 10:48, which comment on the composition of modern Lamanites including the American Indians, Mestizos of Latin America, Polynesians, and so on. Consequently, today's Lamanites should be proud that they have among their progenitors the great prophets through whom the Lord gave the scriptures now included in the Book of Mormon. Note, however, how the Lord consistently refers to the children of Lehi as Lamanites in these and succeeding revelations in the Doctrine and Covenants. (See Chart 2.)

Section 4: Calls to the Work

This was the first of numerous revelations given in response to individuals' having asked Joseph Smith to inquire of the Lord concerning what was to be their part in the restored work. Even though the Lord addressed specific persons in these revelations, in reality he is speaking "to all those who have desires to bring forth and establish this work." (D&C 12:7; see also 11:27 and 93:49.)

"A Marvelous Work" (Verses 1–4). The "marvelous work" refers to the Latter-day restoration, including the publication of the Book of Mormon, organization of the Church, and proclamation of the gospel in its fullness. The prophet Isaiah had anticipated these events long ago; notice how his language is reflected in section 4. (See Isaiah 29:11–14.) The "field" being "white already to harvest" represents the world's readiness to receive the restored gospel. Therefore, those who desire to serve should thrust in their sickle, or in other words, be totally committed and serve "with all your heart, might, mind and strength." (Verse 2.) Great blessings are promised; sharing the gospel with others has the effect of strengthening one's own testimony.

Essential Qualities (Verses 5–7). These verses (together with D&C 12:8) list some of the attributes the Lord considered important for those whom he was calling into his service. Ponder how each of them is likewise essential to success in our present Church callings. The opposites of these qualities (such as fear rather than faith, for example) generally bring failure. (For an excellent discussion see Doxey, *The Doctrine and Covenants Speaks,* vol. 1, chap. 6.)

Many of the ideas originally revealed to Joseph Smith, Sr., in section 4 were subsequently repeated to others who were similarly being called to the work: Oliver Cowdery, D&C 6:1–6; Hyrum Smith, 11:1–6; Joseph Knight, Sr., 12:1–6; and David Whitmer, 14:1–6. The Lord's counsel in these verses placed in proper perspective the specific assignment given to each of these brethren. Notice how he particularly challenged them to "seek to bring forth and establish the cause of Zion." (D&C 6:6, for example.) "Zion" is the name given to the people and city which must be prepared for the Lord's second coming. (See the discussion of sections 57 and

58 for a further consideration of the importance of establishing Zion.)

Joseph Smith, Sr. The Prophet's father, one of the earliest to
receive a testimony of the restored gospel, heeded the counsel
contained in section 4 and thrust in his sickle with his might.
He was one of the Eight Witnesses to the Book of Mormon in
1829, was baptized and confirmed a member of the Church on
April 6, 1830, was ordained Patriarch to the Church in 1833,
served on the first high council in 1834, was called as an assistant counselor in the First Presidency in 1837, endured mob violence in Ohio and Missouri, and died in 1840 a stalwart in the
faith.

Section 5 and Martin Harris

During the previous summer (1828), Martin Harris had
been involved in the loss of 116 pages of Book of Mormon
translation. (See "Section 3 and the Lost Manuscript" herein.) Now repentant, Martin was seeking to learn of his place
in the work in general and whether he might be permitted to
see the Book of Mormon plates in particular.

How Knowledge Comes (Verses 2-29). Martin Harris apparently
was skeptical by nature and therefore frequently sought further evidence. For example, he took a copy of characters
from the Book of Mormon plates to scholars in New York
City for their appraisal. Then he felt the need to show 116
pages of the completed translation to family members in order to convince them. Now he was seeking a further witness
for himself. In section 5 the Lord explained to Martin how a
testimony is and is not obtained. These principles apply likewise to all who are seeking a knowledge of the truth.

The Lord pointed out that those who do not already have
faith would not be convinced even if they could see the
plates. (Verse 7.) Earlier he had promised that "signs" or
tangible manifestations would *follow* those that believe. (See
Mark 16:15-16; for a further consideration of the relationship between signs and faith, see the discussion of D&C
63:7-12.) Instead, the world is to gain a knowledge of the

truth through the living prophet. (Verse 10.) Furthermore, there will be the testimony of other witnesses. Even these selected individuals will know the work is true, not because they see the plates with their physical eyes, but because "from heaven will I declare it unto them." (Verses 11–12.) Still, one must gain a witness for himself. The Lord outlined how this may be accomplished. Those who believe his words (available in the scriptures and through the living prophet and other witnesses) will receive direct and personal manifestations from the Holy Ghost. (Compare verse 16 with Alma's instructions on how to cultivate faith—Alma 32:26–43.) The Spirit can then give us a sure personal knowledge of all things. (Moroni 10:5.) To receive this desired testimony one must humble himself, confess his sins, and covenant to keep the Lord's commandments. (D&C 5:24–28.)

Further Instructions (Verses 30–34). After cautioning Joseph to pause in the work of translation and warning him of Martin's weaknesses, the Lord promised other "means" by which the Prophet could accomplish his assignment. This promise may have been fulfilled the following month with the arrival of Oliver Cowdery, who was to be the Prophet's scribe throughout almost the entire translation project.

Section 6 and the Coming of Oliver Cowdery

While Joseph Smith was still residing in Harmony, Pennsylvania, Oliver Cowdery was teaching school in Palmyra. It was the custom of the day to have the school teacher board with the various families sending children to school. Thus, Oliver came to live with the Smiths, where he first learned about Joseph's work of translating the Book of Mormon plates. After retiring one evening, Oliver prayed for and received a witness from God that these things were true.

When school closed for the season, Oliver decided to go to Harmony and meet the Prophet himself. Oliver arrived in Harmony on April 5, 1829, and started work as Joseph Smith's scribe two days later. He later declared:

I wrote, with my own pen, the entire Book of Mormon (save a few pages) as it fell from the lips of the Prophet Joseph Smith, as he translated it by the gift and power of God, by the means of the Urim and Thummim. ("Journal History," October 21, 1848.)

A Special Testimony for Oliver Cowdery (Verses 14-24). Oliver kept secret the matter of having received a witness from God until after section 6 had been received. The Lord gave Joseph Smith the power to reveal things which were in Oliver's mind in order to confirm the latter's testimony. Notice that together with this special witness he received added responsibility. (Verses 18-19).

Oliver, at that time, stood at the beginning of many years of service in the Lord's kingdom. Oliver also had the privilege of being one of the three special witnesses to the Book of Mormon. No other individual besides Joseph Smith is mentioned more often in the Doctrine and Covenants than is Oliver Cowdery. He served as the Assistant President of the Church from December 5, 1834, until the time of his apostasy and excommunication in 1838. (For a discussion of this office see section 124 herein.) In 1848 he humbly returned to the Church and was rebaptized on November 12. He died as a faithful member on March 3, 1850.

"Seek Not for Riches" (Verse 7). This verse may give the impression that wordly wealth is to be avoided. Such an idea, however, is unreasonable as one recognizes the importance of temporal resources in building the Lord's kingdom on earth. The scriptures teach that money, as such, is not necessarily evil, but that by placing the acquisition of wordly wealth ahead of developing things of the Spirit, one commits sin. Thus, money should not be an end in itself but should be used mostly as a means to do good. One's attitude toward worldly wealth is, therefore, all-important. Consider the teachings in the following passages on the subject: Matthew 6:33; 1 Timothy 6:10; Jacob 2:17-19; D&C 56:16-18.

"The Mysteries of God Shall Be Unfolded unto You" (Verse 7). How is this promise to be reconciled with Joseph Smith's instructions to the elders to "declare the first principles, and let mysteries alone"? (*Teachings,* p. 292.) In the theological sense, a "mystery" might be defined as something which cannot be

known through human faculties alone but must be made known through divine revelation. The Lord has chosen not to give revelation about certain matters; these are the "mysteries" we should leave alone. The student of the gospel should never fear to ask questions; but when he learns that the answer has not been revealed, he should follow Alma's example when he said: "Now these mysteries are not yet fully made known unto me; therefore I shall forbear." (Alma 37:11.) On the other hand, the Lord has consented to reveal fundamental and profound truths including "the mysteries of the kingdom, even the key of the knowledge of God." (D&C 84:19.) Similarly, an understanding of the plan of salvation and of the place of Christ's mission can be obtained only by divine revelation. Such "mysteries" we should earnestly seek to comprehend. D&C 63:22–23 suggests that only the obedient will understand the mysteries, or, in other words, the Lord's will for them.

The Importance of Desire (Verse 8 ff). Notice how many times this and subsequent revelations declare proper desire to be a necessary prerequisite to receiving blessings. (In section 6, for example, see verses 8, 20, 22, 25 and 27.) Just as "faith without works is dead" (James 2:26), more than mere desire is necessary. Oliver Cowdery desired to translate like Joseph Smith and was granted this privilege by which he could bring forth other records containing yet unknown gospel truths. (Verses 25–27.) Nevertheless, as will be seen in section 9, Oliver failed to pay the price, so these promises were never realized.

Further Counsel (Verses 32–37). Compare verse 32 with a similar promise recorded in Matthew 18:20. Notice how in this revelation the Lord stresses the importance of being united. Although the "little flock" might be few in numbers, they should not hesitate to do good. (Verses 33–34.) The invitation in verse 37 to behold the Savior's wounds does not necessarily mean that Joseph and Oliver were privileged to see him on this occasion; rather, this was an admonition for them to remember him and contemplate the meaning of his mission.

Section 7 and John's Desire

This section is the inspired translation of an account written by John the apostle on a parchment. The parchment was not necessarily present physically but was probably seen by revelation. Compare section 7 with John 21:20–23 to see what is added to the knowledge available in the Bible.

John Chapter 21	D&C Section 7
21. Peter seeing him [John] saith to Jesus, Lord, and what shall this man do?	1. And the Lord said unto me: John, my beloved, what desirest thou? For if you shall ask what you will, it shall be granted unto you.
	2. And I said unto him: Lord, give unto me power over death, that I may live and bring souls unto thee.
	3. And the Lord said unto me: . . . because thou desirest this thou shalt tarry until I come in my glory, and shalt prophesy before nations, kindreds, tongues and people.
22. Jesus saith unto him, If I will that he tarry till I come, what is that to thee? follow thou me.	4. And for this cause the Lord said unto Peter: If I will that he tarry till I come, what is that to thee? For he desired of me that he might bring souls unto me, but thou desiredst that thou mightest speedily come unto me in my kingdom.
23. Then went this saying abroad among the brethren, that that disciple should not die: yet Jesus said not unto him, He shall not die; but, If I will that he tarry till I come, what is that to thee?	5. I say unto thee, Peter, this was a good desire; but my beloved has desired that he might do more. . . .

At a conference held June 3–6, 1831, the Prophet Joseph Smith learned by revelation that "John the Revelator was then among the ten tribes of Israel . . . to prepare them for their return from their long dispersion to again possess the land of their fathers." (*HC*, 1:176, footnote.)

Translated Beings. Joseph Smith taught that "translated bodies are designed for future missions." (*Teachings,* p. 191.) For example, Moses and Elijah were to bestow the keys of the priesthood to Peter, James, and John on the Mount of Transfiguration. (*Teachings,* p. 158.) Because this is done by the laying on of hands, Moses and Elijah would need tangible bodies. Since these keys were to be conferred before Christ inaugurated the resurrection, Moses and Elijah had to be blessed in such a way that they might retain their mortal bodies much longer than the normal lifespan. Similarly, John the Revelator (John 21:20–23) and the three Nephite disciples (3 Nephi 28) were "translated" so that they could remain on earth and labor to prepare the world for Christ's second coming.

What is the nature of these translated beings? Joseph Smith observed that many have supposed that translated beings "were taken immediately into the presence of God and into eternal fullness," but that is a mistaken idea. "Their place of habitation is that of the terrestrial order." The Prophet made a distinction between the "actual resurrection and translation: translation obtains deliverance from the tortures and sufferings of the body, but their existence will prolong as to the labors and toils of the ministry, before they can enter into so great a rest and glory." (*Teachings,* pp. 170–71.) "Translated bodies cannot enter into rest until they have undergone a change equivalent to death." (*Teachings,* p. 191.) Consider also the information about the three Nephite disciples in 3 Nephi 28, especially verses 7–9 and 36–40. Mormon noted that a change had already come upon them. They had been quickened from their telestial state to a higher terrestrial level. He then indicated that a greater change would accompany Christ's second coming. These translated beings would then be changed in the twinkling of an eye from mortality to immortality. The three Nephite disciples were promised that they would never "taste of death" nor "endure the pains of death." This did not mean they would never die. Compare this promise with a similar statement in the Doctrine and Covenants (42:46) that the righteous who "die in me shall not taste of death, for it shall be sweet unto them." In light of the above, consider the placement of translated beings on Chart 3.

Chart 3

Types of Bodies

	Spirit	Mortal	Immortal
Celestial	Holy Ghost; (Our preexistence)		Father and Son; resurrected in celestial kingdom
Terrestrial		Translated beings; mortals during millennium	Resurrected in terrestrial kingdom
Telestial		Our present state	Resurrected in telestial kingdom
Sons of Perdition	Those who followed Satan in preexistence		Those who committed unpardonable sin (resurrected)

Sections 8–9 and Oliver's Desire to Translate

"Oliver Cowdery became exceedingly anxious to have the power to translate bestowed upon him" (*HC* 1:36) as had been promised in section 6, verses 25–27. It was in this setting that section 8 was given. The Lord stated that Oliver had two gifts. Apparently Oliver failed to magnify his gift of translation, and section 9 was given to explain his failure. As a result, Oliver forfeited the opportunity he might have otherwise had to translate other ancient records.

Oliver's Gifts (D&C 8:2–9). Oliver Cowdery was reminded that the Holy Ghost is "the spirit of revelation." (Verses 2–3.) Similarly, the Prophet Joseph Smith taught that one cannot receive the Holy Ghost without also receiving revelation. (*Teachings*, p. 238.)

The exact nature of the "gift of Aaron" is not known. Some have suggested that this gift gave Oliver Cowdery power to be the mouthpiece for Joseph Smith, even as Aaron had been for Moses. Oliver was subsequently called to be the "first preacher of this church." (D&C 21:11–12.) It should be remembered, however, that Sidney Rigdon was later called by revelation to be the spokesman for Joseph Smith. (D&C 100:9–11.) Other students point out that in the original Book of Commandments this gift is referred to as "the rod of Aaron"; the idea that there may have been a tangible sacred instrument present is sustained by the promise in verse 8 of section 8 that Oliver would "hold it in [his] hands." (Sperry, *Compendium,* p. 71.)

Oliver's Failure (Section 9). Many have supposed that Oliver Cowdery failed when he attempted to translate. Section 9, however, indicates that he did commence to translate but then quit because of fear (verses 5 and 11) and so resumed his more comfortable role as scribe (verse 1). He therefore lost the privilege to translate because of his lack of faith. (Compare Oliver's experience with that of Peter when he commenced to walk upon the water—Matthew 14:22–31.)

Getting Answers to Prayers (D&C 9:7–9). This passage describes the process known as "spiritual confirmation." The individual takes the initiative by studying the matter out in his own mind first, and then by asking the Lord if his conclusions are

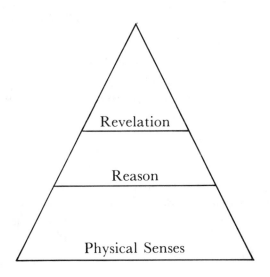

right. The process is complete only when the individual is able to recognize the Lord's answer.

Epistemology is the branch of philosophy which considers how one can know the truth. Over the centuries, scholars have debated the relative roles of the physical senses and reason in gaining knowledge. The scriptures frequently refer to *seeing* or *hearing* the truth. Furthermore, the Lord promised Oliver Cowdery that he would reveal the truth to Oliver Cowdery in his *mind* as well as in his heart. (D&C 8:2.) The revelation in section 9 indicates that divine revelation must be added to the physical senses and reason as the ultimate source of truth.

Section 10: Satan's Plan Thwarted

Exactly when section 10 was received is not known. All editions of the Doctrine and Covenants prior to 1921 gave the date as May 1829. When Elder B. H. Roberts edited Joseph Smith's *History of the Church* early in the twentieth century, he regarded this date as an error. Elder Roberts cited the statement in Joseph Smith's history that section 10 was received "a few days" after section 3 had been given. (*HC,* 1:23.) Even though the present edition of the Doctrine and Covenants has changed the date of section 10 to "summer of 1828," this revelation remains where it would appear chronologically if the date were May 1829. (See also the discussion of section 3 herein.)

Satan's Plan (Verses 10-19). Had Joseph Smith retranslated the lost material, Satan would have prompted the Prophet's enemies to alter the wording in the missing original so as to discredit the translator. Attempting to translate 116 pages word-for-word exactly the same a second time would have been "tempting" the Lord. (Verse 15.) One generally translates ideas rather than words. Furthermore, the Lord has indicated that he gives revelations—including inspired translations—to his servants "after the manner of their language." (D&C 1:24.) Thus it would not have been appropriate to criticize Joseph Smith even if he had failed to translate with identical wording a second time.

Satan's Tactics (Verses 19–28). Satan not only wants to thwart the work of God, but he also wants to destroy the souls of men and make them miserable like himself. (Compare verse 22 with 2 Nephi 2:27.) His tactics, as described in this revelation and in 2 Nephi 28:20–22, can be recognized on all sides in today's world.

The Lord's Counterplan (Verses 30–46). In order to comprehend Satan's plan to frustrate the coming forth of the Book of Mormon and to appreciate the Lord's counterplan, an understanding of the nature of the two sets of Book of Mormon plates is essential. Nephi made two sets of plates "for a wise purpose in the Lord." (1 Nephi 9:5.) On the Small Plates of Nephi, the prophets gave a religious history covering the period from 600 B.C. to about 150 B.C., when they were filled up. The first six books of the present Book of Mormon were translated from the Small Plates. The kings kept a political and military history on the Large Plates of Nephi. The book of Lehi covers roughly the same period as the Small Plates. The book of Mosiah, which followed the book of Lehi on the Large Plates, inaugurated a combined religious and secular history which continued to the time of Mormon, who prepared an abridgment of the Large Plates. (See Chart 4.)

Joseph Smith began his work by translating from Mormon's abridgment, and it was the manuscript translation of the book of Lehi which Martin Harris lost. In section 10, verses 38–46, the Lord instructed Joseph Smith not to retranslate the book of Lehi taken originally from the political history on the Large Plates, but rather to translate the Small Plates covering the same period of time and throwing a greater light on the gospel of Jesus Christ. (See verses 39–40.) Then the Prophet was to continue translating from the Large Plates, beginning with the book of Mosiah, which also contained things of the Spirit. (See verses 41 and 46.) In light of these instructions, consider the net results of losing the manuscript. To what extent was the Lord's work frustrated? Note that the Book of Lehi was a purely secular history; none of the religious history was lost.

Chart 4
Book of Mormon
Time Span of Books and Pages
Compiled by Richard O. Cowan.
Adapted from *The Instructor*, December 1962

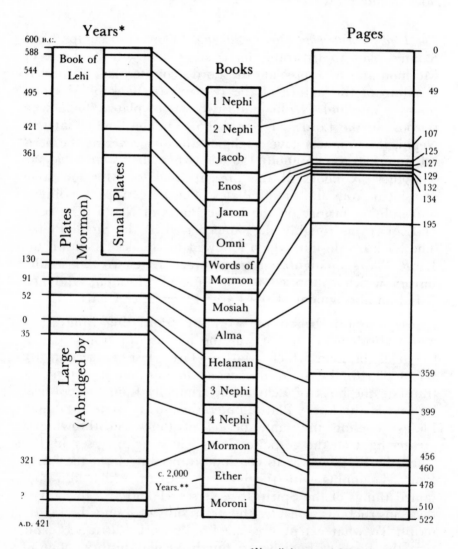

*Not all dates are definitely known.
**See Ether 1; 13:20-22; Omni 21.

The Lord's Church vs. the Kingdom of Satan (Verses 53–69). Doctrine and Covenants 1:30 declares that there is but "one true and living church." Section 10 (particularly verse 67) defines the attributes of those who can claim membership in the Lord's church. These qualities are in marked contrast to the behavior advocated by Satan (described above).

Section 11

According to Joseph Smith's history, section 13 preceded section 11 in chronological order. Following the restoration of the Aaronic Priesthood, two of the Prophet's brothers came from Palmyra to Harmony to learn more about his work. Samuel H. Smith was baptized May 25, 1829. Not many days afterward, Hyrum Smith also arrived; section 11 was received for him. Hyrum was subsequently baptized during the month of June. (See *HC*, 1:45.) Note particularly the Lord's counsel to Hyrum regarding preparation for his mission.

Hyrum Smith. The oldest surviving brother of Joseph Smith, Hyrum was born February 9, 1800. These two brothers enjoyed an especially close relationship. Joseph wrote: "Hyrum, thy name shall be written in the *Book of the Law of the Lord,* for those who come after thee to look upon, that they may pattern after thy works." (*HC*, 5:108.) The Lord also declared his love for Hyrum. (See D&C 124:15.) Hyrum became one of the Eight Witnesses to the Book of Mormon just a few weeks after this revelation was received. He was also called as second counselor in the First Presidency on November 7, 1837; and on January 24, 1841, the Lord appointed him Assistant President and Patriarch to the Church. (D&C 124:91–96.) He capped his earthly mission by sharing the martyr's crown with his brother Joseph. (See D&C 135:3.)

Becoming the Children of God (Verse 30). The scriptures apply the title "father" to members of the Godhead in at least four distinct senses:

1. Father as literal parent. All people are actually the spirit sons or daughters of Elohim (God the Eternal Father). Jesus Christ is known as the "Firstborn" because he was the eldest of God's spirit children. In addition, the Savior was

Hyrum Smith (Photo courtesy Harold B. Lee Library)

the Only Begotten Son of God in the flesh through the miracle of the virgin birth.

2. Father as creator. Even though Jesus Christ was the Son of God, he is sometimes called the "Father of heaven and earth" because he was the Creator. (See Mosiah 3:8; Helaman 14:12; John 1:10; Hebrews 1:1–3.) Similarly, Eli Whitney may be called the "father" of the cotton gin or George Washington may be called the "father of his country."

3. Father of the faithful by adoption. Even though men are already the spirit offspring of God, they may become his children in still another sense. Even as one's mortal parents made physical birth possible, so also is being "born again" spiritually made possible through the atonement of Jesus Christ. King Benjamin directed those who had just received a witness through the Spirit that "because of the covenant which ye have made ye shall be called the children of Christ, his sons, and his daughters; for behold, this day he hath spiritually begotten you; for ye say that your hearts are changed through faith on his name; therefore, ye are born of him and have become his sons and his daughters." (Mosiah 5:7.) It was in this sense that the promise in Doctrine and Covenants 11:30 was given. (See also John 1:12; D&C 25:1; 35:1–2; 39:1–4.)

4. Father by divine investiture of authority. The Son has on occasion appeared as the authorized representative of the Father and so has been received as though he were the Father. (See John 5:43.) Similarly, John received an angel who came in the name of the Lord as though he were the Savior himself. (See Revelation 1:1; 22:8–9.)

(For a further discussion of the subject, read "The Father and Son: A Doctrinal Exposition by the First Presidency and the Twelve," quoted in James E. Talmage, *Articles of Faith,* Appendix 2:11.)

Section 12

Joseph Knight, Sr., of Colesville, New York, was the head of a family which was to play an important part in the Church. Even though he had not yet been baptized, he believed in the truthfulness of Joseph Smith's work and on several occasions traveled the thirty miles from Colesville to Harmony to bring provisions to help the Prophet. In Section 23, Joseph Knight was directed by revelation to join the Church, which he did shortly afterward. (For further consideration of the ideas in this revelation, see the discussion under section 4 herein.)

Section 13: Restoration of the Aaronic Priesthood

In the Prophet's history, section 13 was recorded chronologically before section 11. Read the entire account of the restoration of the Aaronic Priesthood in the Pearl of Great Price, JSH 1:68-75. John the Baptist, last in a long series of Aaronic Priesthood bearers, was privileged to prepare the way for and to baptize the Savior. (See D&C 84:26-28; Matthew 3:13-17. For a consideration of the history and scope of the Aaronic and Melchizedek priesthoods, see the discussion of section 107 herein.)

The statement that the priesthood will remain "until . . ." does not mean that it will be withdrawn at some future time. (Compare D&C 84:18.) When Oliver Cowdery recorded John the Baptist's words, he quoted the heavenly messenger as saying that the priesthood must remain "that the Sons of Levi may yet offer an offering unto the Lord in righteousness." (Quoted in the Pearl of Great Price, 1981 edition, p. 58 fn.)

The identity of the "Sons of Levi" and of their "offering" can be understood in two senses: First, literal descendants of Levi will return with the Ten Tribes before the Second Coming and will make an actual blood sacrifice as a necessary token of the "restoration of all things." (See *Teachings*, p. 172.) Second, in a more figurative sense, Doctrine and Covenants 84:33-34 indicates that faithful bearers of the Aaronic and Melchizedek priesthoods become the sons of Aaron and of Moses respectively; they thus become the "Sons of Levi" because Aaron and Moses were both descendants of Levi. The "offering" given by these faithful Latter-day Saints may include "a broken heart and a contrite spirit" (3 Nephi 9:19-20) as well as an acceptable record of their dead. (D&C

128:24.) (For a further consideration of the Sons of Levi and their offering, see Sperry, *Compendium,* pp. 74–84.)

Sections 14–16 and the Whitmers of Fayette

While Oliver Cowdery was teaching school in Palmyra during the winter of 1828–29, he met and became a close friend of David Whitmer. At the end of the school term, Oliver decided to go to Harmony, Pennsylvania, where he could meet Joseph Smith personally. (For circumstances see the discussion of section 6.) On his way he visited the Whitmers in Fayette, promising to write them and give his impressions of the Prophet.

Almost immediately Oliver went to work as Joseph's scribe. By the first of June 1829, opposition in Harmony mounted, and the work of translation was increasingly harassed. In these circumstances the Prophet was glad to accept the Whitmers' invitation for him and Oliver to go to Fayette; the family offered to provide not only free room and board, but also to assist as scribes in the work of translation as well.

Some remarkable spiritual manifestations accompanied Joseph's move to Fayette—a fitting beginning for the significant relationship that was to exist between the Prophet and the Whitmer family. (See map on pp. 8–9. For more details, see B. H. Roberts, *Comprehensive History of the Church,* 1:124; and Lucy Mack Smith, *History of the Prophet Joseph Smith* [Salt Lake City: The Improvement Era, 1902], chap. 30.)

Section 17 and the Three Witnesses

In previous revelations the Lord had suggested to three individuals that they might be privileged to stand with Joseph Smith as eyewitnesses of the Book of Mormon plates: Martin Harris (D&C 5:11–13, 24–28; note the discussion of the witnesses' responsibilities), Oliver Cowdery (D&C 6:25–28), and David Whitmer (D&C 14:8). As the work of translation drew to a close, these three men became very eager to be the special witnesses spoken of in the record.

The revelation in section 17 assured the three that through

The three witnesses of the Book of Mormon (Photo courtesy Harold B. Lee Library)

their faith and by the power of God they would see not only the plates, but four other sacred objects as well. The Lord also warned the witnesses that it would be their responsibility to sustain Joseph Smith with their testimony.

Not many days after this revelation was received, Joseph Smith was present at the customary morning devotional service in the Whitmer home. In great solemnity he declared:

Martin Harris, you have got to humble yourself before your God this day, that you may obtain a forgiveness of your sins. If you do, it is the will of God that you should look upon the plates, in company with Oliver Cowdery and David Whitmer. (Lucy Mack Smith, *History of the Prophet Joseph Smith,* chap. 31.)

The Prophet then recorded what happened the same day:

We four, viz., Martin Harris, David Whitmer, Oliver Cowdery and myself, agreed to retire into the woods, and try to obtain, by fervent and humble prayer, the fulfillment of the promises given in the above revelation—that they should have a view of the plates. We accordingly made choice of a piece of woods convenient to Mr. Whitmer's house, to which we retired, and having knelt down, we began to pray in much faith to Almighty God to bestow upon us a realization of these promises.

According to previous arrangement, I commenced by vocal prayer to our Heavenly Father, and was followed by each of the others in succession. We did not at the first trial, however, obtain any answer or manifestation of divine favor in our behalf. We again observed the same order of prayer, each calling on and praying fervently to God in rotation, but with the same result as before.

Upon this, our second failure, Martin Harris proposed that he should withdraw himself from us, believing, as he expressed himself, that his presence was the cause of our not obtaining what we wished for. He accordingly withdrew from us, and we knelt down again, and had not been many minutes engaged in prayer, when presently we beheld a light above us in the air, of exceeding brightness; and behold, an angel stood before us. In his hands he held the plates which we had been praying for these to have a view of. He turned over the leaves one by one, so that we could see them, and discern the engravings thereon distinctly. He then addressed himself to David Whitmer, and

said, "David, blessed is the Lord, and he that keeps His commandments"; when, immediately afterwards, we heard a voice from out of
the bright light above us, saying, "These plates have been revealed by
the power of God, and they have been translated by the power of God.
The translation of them which you have seen is correct, and I command you to bear record of what you now see and hear."

I now left David and Oliver, and went in pursuit of Martin Harris, whom I found at a considerable distance, fervently engaged in
prayer. He soon told me, however, that he had not yet prevailed with
the Lord, and earnestly requested me to join him in prayer, that he
also might realize the same blessings which we had just received.

We accordingly joined in prayer, and ultimately obtained our desires,
for before we had yet finished, the same vision was opened to our view,
at least it was again opened to me, and I once more beheld and heard
the same things; whilst at the same moment, Martin Harris cried out,
apparently in an ecstasy of joy, " 'Tis enough; 'tis enough; mine eyes
have beheld; mine eyes have beheld;" and jumping up, he shouted,
"Hosanna," blessing God, and otherwise rejoiced exceedingly. (HC,
1:54–55.)

Concerning their experience, David Whitmer wrote many
years later:

In the midst of this light . . . there appeared, as it were, a table with
many records or plates upon it, besides the plates of the Book of Mormon, also the sword of Laban, the Directors [or Liahona] and the In-
terpreters [or Urim and Thummim]. . . . I also heard the voice of the
Lord, as distinctly as I ever heard anything in my life, declaring that
the records of the plates of the Book of Mormon were translated by the
gift and power of God. (B. H. Roberts, New Witness for God, vol.
2, pp. 271–314.)

Thus the promises in section 17 were literally fulfilled.

It was mid-afternoon when the brethren returned to the
house. The Prophet's mother recalled that:

On coming in Joseph threw himself down beside me, and exclaimed:
"Father, mother, you do not know how happy I am; the Lord has now
caused the plates to be shown to three more besides myself. They have

seen an angel, who has testified to them, and they will have to bear witness to the truth of what I have said, for now they know for themselves that I do not go about to deceive the people, and I feel as if I was relieved of a burden which was almost too heavy for me to bear, and it rejoices my soul, that I am not any longer to be entirely alone in the work." Upon this Martin Harris came in. He seemed almost overcome with joy, and testified boldly to what he had both seen and heard. And so did David and Oliver, adding, that no tongue could express the joy of their hearts, and the greatness of the things which they had both seen and heard. (Lucy Mack Smith, *History of the Prophet Joseph Smith*, chap. 31.)

Even though all three of these witnesses later left the Church because of personal differences with Joseph Smith, none of them ever denied their testimony despite ridicule and scorn which was often directed at them. Two of the three subsequently repented and reunited with the Saints.

As one compares the testimony of the Three Witnesses with that of the group of Eight Witnesses, it is instructive to contrast the supernatural experience of the former with the more natural and yet still significant experience of the latter. The Three Witnesses were shown the plates by an angel who turned the pages for their examination, and they heard the voice of God bearing testimony of the work. The Eight Witnesses, on the other hand, "handled" and "hefted" the plates which were shown them by Joseph Smith himself. Both types of witnesses are important to satisfy a variety of people.

Section 18 and the Authority to Preach

Verses 2–8 were directed primarily to Oliver Cowdery. (Compare section 6.) Beginning with verse 9, this revelation was addressed to both Oliver Cowdery and David Whitmer.

Call to Preach the Gospel (Verses 9–25). Verse 9 reminded Oliver Cowdery and David Whitmer that they had the same calling as Paul the apostle. The Lord told these brethren that their basic responsibility was to preach repentance (verse 14), because each individual is a child of God and, therefore, "the worth of souls is great in the sight of God" (verse 10). Not only does the Savior rejoice in the soul that repents, thereby qualifying for the Lord's greatest blessings (verses 11–13), but the missionaries will also receive great joy in the kingdom of heaven *with* those whom they bring to repentance (see verses 15–16). The Lord had earlier given similar instructions and made similar promises to two other Whitmer brothers in identical revelations. (See sections 15 and 16, verses 6.) The missionaries were, therefore, counseled not to waste their time in fruitless debate over theological tenets of specific churches, but to stress the first principles of the gospel. (See D&C 18:20; 19:31.)

Restoration of the Melchizedek Priesthood. Peter, James, and John restored the higher or Melchizedek Priesthood in fulfillment of the promise made by John the Baptist when he restored the Aaronic Priesthood. Even though it is known where the restoration took place, the record of the exact date of this important event has been lost. It is not known whether or not this priesthood had been restored by the time section 18 had been received, although many students of the Doctrine and Covenants believe that verse 9 indicates that Oliver Cowdery and David Whitmer did have the Melchizedek Priesthood by that time.

It is possible to approximate the time of the restoration in the light of the following evidence. The Melchizedek Priesthood was restored on the banks of the Susquehanna River in the "wilderness" between Harmony, Pennsylvania, and Colesville, New York. (See D&C 128:20 and map on pp. 8–9.) Joseph Smith and Oliver Cowdery left the Susquehanna River country and moved about 100 miles to Fayette about June 1, 1829, "and there resided until the translation [of the Book of Mormon] was finished" (*HC,* 1:48–49). Joseph Smith recorded that in June 1829, "We now became anxious to have that promise realized to us, which the angel that conferred upon us the Aaronic Priesthood had given us, viz., that provided we continued faithful, we should also have the Melchizedek Priesthood. ... We had for some time made this matter a subject of humble prayer, and at length we got together in the chamber of Mr. Whitmer's house, in order more particularly to seek of the Lord what we now so earnestly desired." The Lord directed Joseph and Oliver to ordain each other elders, but to defer this action until a time when others who had been baptized could meet together and vote as to whether or not they would sanction these proceedings; this meeting was held on April 6, 1830, when the Church was officially organized. (See *HC,* 1:60–62.)

In addition to restoring the Melchizedek Priesthood itself, Peter, James, and John also restored keys necessary to organize the Lord's kingdom. (See D&C 27:12–13; 128:20.)

"Search Out the Twelve" (Verses 26–39). In these verses the Lord told his servants how they could recognize those who were to become apostles, and he gave instructions to the future Twelve. This commandment was fulfilled nearly six years later when, on February 14, 1835, the original Twelve Apostles were called and ordained. Even though only Oliver Cowdery and David Whitmer are here appointed to "search out the Twelve," Martin Harris was also included later, so that all three special witnesses of the Book of Mormon participated in the selection of the original Twelve.

Section 19

Mr. Egbert B. Grandin, who was printing the Book of Mormon in Palmyra, stopped work on the nearly completed project when a group of townspeople voted to refrain from purchasing the book if it were published. It was in this setting that the Lord directed Martin Harris in section 19 to pay in advance the agreed upon price of $3,000. (See verses 13–16, 20, 25–26, 34–35.) This Martin did at great personal sacrifice.

Section 19, however, goes far beyond these circumstances. In order to impress Martin Harris with the importance of keeping this commandment, the Lord elucidated the relationship among the Atonement, repentance, and the forgiveness of sins.

Eternal Punishment (Verses 4–12). In order to comprehend why punishment is necessary, one must understand the principle of *justice.* God operates according to law, obedience to which will always bring blessings (D&C 130:20–21), but disobedience to which brings punishment (Alma 42:22; 2 Nephi 9:25–27). Thus, punishment is an inevitable consequence of transgression.

God's Laws

Our Choice:	Obedience	or Disobedience
A Condition of:	Righteousness	or Wickedness, Sin
Which Results In:	Blessings	or Punishment, Cursings
Bringing Us:	Happiness, Joy	or Suffering, Sorrow

It is impossible to reconcile God's justice with the erroneous idea that some of his children are saved in heaven but that the majority are condemned to suffer with the devil forever. According to the teachings of the Doctrine and Covenants, "eternal punishment" may be considered "eternal" in three senses:

1. Because "Endless" and "Eternal" are among God's titles, the punishment inflicted under his law may be called *Endless* or *Eternal* punishment, or in other words, *Eternal's* punishment. (See D&C 19:10–11.)

2. God's law is eternal, and according to the principle of justice, punishment must always follow when the law is broken. Thus, punishment is an eternal institution. This may be compared to a prison which is relatively permanent even though individuals come and go, serving sentences only in proportion to the seriousness of their offenses.

3. A few, who become sons of perdition, will actually suffer "eternal punishment" eternally because their offenses are unpardonable; thus, they have placed themselves permanently beyond the possibility of ever again enjoying God's presence or glory. (See D&C 76:44.) The majority, however, will suffer "eternal punishment" only temporarily, until the demands of justice are satisfied according to the number and seriousness of their sins.

Atonement of Jesus Christ (Verses 16–19). According to the principle of mercy, another person, if he is *willing* and *able,* may pay the penalties resulting from our sins. He must make this payment, however, in such a way as not to rob justice (Alma 42:22–25); he, therefore, must require something of us in order for us to qualify for the payment he is making in our behalf.

Because of his great love for us, Jesus Christ was *willing* to make the atoning sacrifice in our behalf. He was *able* to do so because of his own sinlessness, which gave him power over spiritual death, and because his being the Son of an Immortal Father and of a mortal mother gave him unique powers over the physical death. The Savior's death and resurrection made it possible for all mankind to be resurrected. (See 1 Corinthians 15:21–22.) When he suffered in the Garden of Gethsemane and on the cross, he paid the penalty for our individual sins; thus, each of us owes a personal debt of gratitude to the Lord for opening the way for us to receive salvation and exaltation.

When penalties for sin are paid, either through one's own suffering or through the atonement of Jesus Christ, the demands of justice are satisfied and *pardon* is achieved. *Forgiveness,* on the other hand, refers specifically to Christ's assuming the burden of paying the penalties of sin for those who repent. (See Chart 5.)

Faith in the Lord Jesus Christ is the first step in the gospel, because it is only through his atonement that salvation is possible. Repentance then follows logically as the individual learns that obedience to divine law is required if sins are to be forgiven through the atonement; this is why one must repent or suffer—that is, pay the punishment of his own sins which would cause the individual to suffer even as Christ suffered. (See D&C 19:16–18.) Furthermore, as the individual becomes better acquainted with Christ, he will be motivated to pattern his own life after the Lord's example. Finally, inasmuch as sin is the main obstacle in the way of achieving spiritual goals, repentance is the means of removing the problem. Through baptism, the individual covenants to obey God's commandments and receives remission of his sins. Receiving the Holy Ghost completely cleanses the individual from the effects of sin and brings him back into direct communion with the Godhead. (See the discussion of justification and sanctification, under section 20.)

Chart 5

Repent Or Suffer
The Two Roads to Pardon

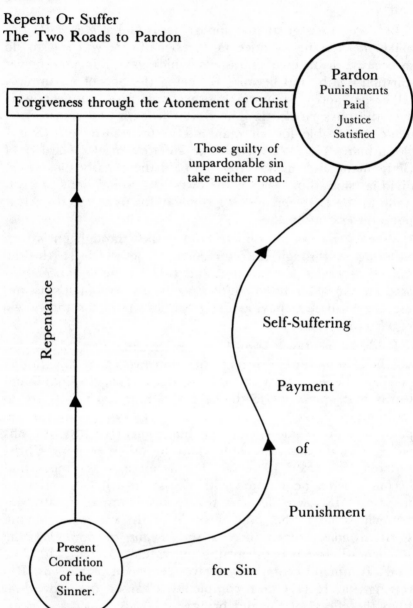

The Lamanites—A Remnant of the Jews (Verse 27). Today's Lamanites may be called "Jews" in two senses:

1. Lehi and his colony had been "Jews" by citizenship because they had lived in Jerusalem in the kingdom of Judah.

2. After the Nephites had been in the American hemisphere for almost three hundred years, they met and united with the people of Zarahemla or so-called Mulekites. This latter group, including members of the tribe of Judah, had left Jerusalem not long after Lehi had also come to the New World. As previously noted, the Nephites and Lamanites subsequently lived for long periods of time as one people, so that today's Lamanites are not only blood descendants of the original Nephites and Lamanites, but also have some Jewish blood brought to the New World through the Mulekites. (See "The Book of Mormon and the Lamanites" under section 3 herein.)

Section 20: The "Constitution of the Church"

In Joseph Smith's day, churches customarily issued creeds or platforms setting forth basic doctrinal beliefs, procedures, and standards of conduct for the benefit of members or prospective converts. As early as 1829, Joseph Smith and Oliver Cowdery were preparing by "the spirit of prophecy and revelation" such a document for the Restored Church. Section 20, together with section 22, was formally accepted as "The Articles and Covenants of the Church of Christ" at the Church's first conference held June 9, 1830. (*Far West Record,* p. 1.)

Verses 1–36 constitute the testimony of the "first elders" concerning key events leading up to the organization of the Church and concerning important doctrines revealed in the Book of Mormon. Verses 37–84 present instructions on the duties of Church officers and on gospel ordinances. Italicized headings in verses 37, 38, and 68 introduce various divisions of these instructions. Because of the fundamental and comprehensive nature of the contents of this revelation, it has been called the "Constitution of the Church."

Testimony of Joseph and Oliver (Verses 1-36)

When Was Jesus Christ Born? (Verse 1). Although Christians commemorate December 25 as the date of the Lord's birth, most biblical scholars agree that the Savior could not have been born in December because shepherds would not have been out at night with their flocks during that part of the year. Many suggest spring as a more probable time. This is in accordance with the instructions in Doctrine and Covenants 20:1 that the Church should be organized on Tuesday, April 6, 1830, eighteen hundred and thirty years from the time when the Savior had come in the flesh.

Evidence from the Book of Mormon also confirms that Christ was born during the spring. When the Nephites saw signs of his birth, they began counting their years from that event. (See 3 Nephi 2:8.) Almost exactly thirty-three years later, on the fourth day of the first month in the thirty-fourth year, the sign of the crucifixion was seen. (See 3 Nephi 8:5.) This meant that the Lord was born and later died at the same time of the year. The New Testament records that his crucifixion occurred at the time of the Passover, a Jewish holiday celebrated during the early spring. All these pieces of evidence lead to the conclusion that Jesus Christ was born during the early spring. In this sense, the Book of Mormon and the Doctrine and Covenants stand as witnesses for each other.

Coming Forth of the Book of Mormon (Verses 5-16). Many of the early revelations now included in the Doctrine and Covenants were related to the coming forth of the Book of Mormon. Verse 9 states that the Book of Mormon contains "the fulness of the gospel of Jesus Christ." The Book of Mormon may not discuss some doctrines in as much detail as does the Doctrine and Covenants, for example, but it presents the basic principles of the gospel in a clearer, more beautiful, more powerful way than almost anywhere else in the scriptures.

According to verse 11, the Book of Mormon is a witness for the latter-day Restoration as well as for the Bible. It may be recalled that Hyrum Smith was counseled to postpone his preaching until the Book of Mormon had been translated. (See D&C 11:16-19.) In 1831 the elders were commanded to preach from the Book of Mormon as well as from the Bible. (See D&C 42:12.) Some time later the Lord rebuked the Church for overlooking the teachings contained in the former. (See D&C 84:54-58.) Students of the Doctrine and Covenants, therefore, should also seek to obtain a strong testimony of the truthfulness of the Book of Mormon.

Unity of the Godhead (Verse 28). Scriptural statements that the Father, Son, and Holy Ghost are *one* cannot mean that they are physically one person. The circumstances of Christ's baptism (Matthew 3:15-17), his promise to ask the Father to send the Holy Ghost (John 14:16, 26), and Stephen's vision of the Father and the Son (Acts 7:55-56) all indicate that the three members of the Godhead are separate individuals. On numerous occasions, the Savior prayed to his Father. (See, for example, Matthew 26:21.) On one such occasion he prayed that all believers might be *one* even as he and the Father were *one*. (John 17:20-32.) Therefore, the oneness of the Father, Son, and Holy Ghost refers to their being united in purpose, teachings, etc. President Joseph Fielding Smith has suggested that it might be clearer to think in terms of the three being one Godhead. (See *Answers to Gospel Questions,* vol. 1, p. 2.)

Justification, Sanctification, and Grace (Verses 30-32). These terms may sound foreign to many Latter-day Saints, and yet these doctrines are at the heart of the gospel. *Justification* is a judicial act by which the Lord grants remission of sins, releasing the individual from legal condemnation upon condition of faith, repentance, and baptism. This "preparatory gospel" is administered by the lesser priesthood. (See D&C 84:26-27.) It is a preparation for the greater change which is to follow: sanctification.

The terms *sanctification* and *saint* are both derived from the Latin word *sanctus* meaning holy. *Sanctification* is the process by which one becomes holy and pure or, in other words, becomes a *saint* in the fullest sense of that word. This is accomplished by experiencing the baptism of fire and the Holy

Ghost (verse 41) made possible by one's own worthiness and through the authority of the Melchizedek Priesthood.

Grace refers to that which is received from God as a gift—the gospel, Atonement, resurrection, etc. Some have perverted the biblical teaching that salvation comes by the grace of Christ (Ephesians 2:8-9) and teach that men are saved by grace alone. The Book of Mormon has the correct concept in the teaching that "it is by grace that we are saved, after all we can do." (2 Nephi 25:23). *Grace* thus refers to a gift, but one which cannot be received unless the recipient qualifies. (See Hebrews 5:9; James 2:17; also D&C Commentary, pp. 103-104.)

Covenant of Baptism (Verse 37)

This covenant is a three-way agreement involving the individual, the Church, and the Lord. This verse and also Alma's teachings on this subject in Mosiah 18:8-10 are among the clearest explanations of the requirements for baptism and the content of the covenant made at baptism and renewed by partaking of the sacrament.

Priesthood Duties and Official Procedures (Verses 38-67, 80-84)

Four Basic Priesthood Offices (Verses 38-59). When the Church was organized on April 6, 1830, it included only four priesthood offices: deacons, teachers, priests, and elders. (Joseph Smith and Oliver Cowdery had been given the authority of the apostleship, but this was not a formal office in the Church until 1835.) Section 20 outlines the duties assigned to each office; consider how priesthood responsibilities are accumulative as one progresses from office to office. Instructions to "watch over the Church always" and "visit the house of each member, and exhort them to pray vocally and in secret and attend to all family duties" (verses 47, 53) are at the heart of the home teaching and family home evening programs. The basic responsibility to preach and exhort is consistent with the Lord's instructions to various individuals in earlier revelations.

Ordination by the Power of the Holy Ghost (Verse 60). One must hold the priesthood in order to ordain another. However, he who represents the Lord through exercising his priesthood should seek to know the Lord's will before acting; such information comes through the ministration of the Holy Ghost. Thus, priesthood and the influence of the Holy Ghost are related, both being manifestations of God's power. Moroni taught the same principle. (See Moroni 3:4.)

Conferences (Verses 61–62, 81). Conferences conducted by the authorities of the Church were to be attended by the representatives of local branches for the purpose of transacting necessary business. According to these instructions, the early Saints met in conferences every three months. Only after Church membership had become larger and more scattered did a distinction emerge between general conferences and stake conferences. Emphasis at stake conferences is still on providing training for local leaders.

Certificates and Licenses (Verses 63–64). A certificate is a statement attesting that one has been ordained to the priesthood. A license is given by those who hold the keys, directing one to exercise his priesthood in a specified manner; thus temple recommends or missionary certificates are examples of *licenses* as section 20 uses that term.

Common Consent (Verse 65). Church officers are nominated by those in authority through inspiration. Church members have the right to accept or reject but will be held accountable for their decisions, so should make them in the spirit of prayer and fasting. (See D&C 26:2; 28:13.)

President J. Reuben Clark, Jr., explained that:

In this Church, the power of "nominating" or calling to office, is not in the body of the Church. This power is vested in the General Authorities of the Church, and in final analysis in the President of the Church who comes to his place under the guidance of inspired revelation. . . . When the presiding authority has so "nominated" or chosen, or called any man to office, that man is then presented to the body of the Church to be "sustained," in political language to be "elected."

Thus the body of the Church has no "calling" or "nominating" power, but only the sustaining, or politically speaking, the "electing" power. (CR, October 1940, pp. 28–29.)

Continued Development (Verses 66–67). Verses 65–67 were added to this section in the 1835 edition of the Doctrine and Covenants. Reference to bishops, high priests, and high councilors reflects the expansion in Church organization which had occurred since 1830. This is an example of integrating later inspired material into an earlier revelation to bring it up to date rather than listing the new material as a separate revelation.

Was the Restoration of the Church Complete in 1830? It is not wholly accurate to say that the Church was restored on April 6, 1830. Only four priesthood offices—deacon, teacher, priest, and elder—were included in the Church at the time of its organization. The Doctrine and Covenants reflects subsequent expansion of the Church organization. By revelation (D&C 41:9) Edward Partridge was appointed to be the first bishop in the Church. A second bishop was later appointed (D&C 72:8), establishing the pattern of a plurality of bishops working under the direction of one presiding bishop. Section 90 directed the organization of the First Presidency in 1833. Section 102 is an extract from the minutes of the meeting at which the high council was organized, completing the establishment of the first stake of the Church at Kirtland, Ohio, on February 17, 1834. The month of February 1835 witnessed the organization of the Council of the Twelve and the calling of the First Quorum of the Seventy; section 107 was given shortly afterward to instruct these new officers in their duties. The first high priests were ordained in 1831, and the first patriarch set apart in 1833. (Joseph Fielding Smith, *Essentials in Church History,* pp. 126, 168.) (See Chart 14 on page 161.) Missions, wards, auxiliaries, and regions were added even later. It is the conviction of the present writer that as long as a living prophet is guiding the Church, the restoration will continue.

Membership Records (Verses 80–84). Moroni explained that a record of members should be kept "that they might be re-

membered and nourished." (Moroni 6:4.) The method outlined in these verses was suited to the small membership of
the early 1830s. Other procedures, including the use of com-
puters, have been adopted as the Church expanded worldwide. This illustrates how programs may change while principles and purposes remain constant.

Gospel Ordinances and the Duties of Members (Verses 68-79)

Preparation for Baptism (Verses 68-71). Verse 68 may imply
that new members are to be taught following baptism but
before confirmation. The first phrase in the verse is actually
a caption referring not only to verse 68 but to the following
several verses as well. It, therefore, is not part of the thought
contained in the remainder of the verse. Thus, verse 68 directs that converts should be taught before being confirmed.
Ideally, these instructions should also precede baptism.

Verse 71 indicates that one cannot be baptized until he
reaches the "years of accountability," later defined by the
Lord as eight years. (See D&C 68:25-28.) Rather than being
baptized, little children are to be blessed by the elders.
(Verse 70. For a further discussion of the status of little children, see section 29 herein.)

Mode of Baptism (Verses 72-74). The teachings of these verses
and 3 Nephi 11:22-26 are much clearer and more specific
than those in the Bible. Both the Book of Mormon and the
Doctrine and Covenants were intended to come forth as part
of the Restoration, so they would be expected to have more
precise instruction on baptism than does the New Testament,
which was largely written to encourage those who were already members of the church. Nevertheless, the Bible does
include evidence that immersion was the mode of baptism
accepted by the primitive church. (Consider Matthew
3:15-17; John 3:23; Romans 6:3-5.) Keep in mind that the
Greek word *baptizo* refers to immersion.

The Sacrament and Sacrament Meetings (Verses 75-79). The
Saints were to "meet together often" to partake of the sacrament (D&C 20:75; 59:12) and to "instruct and edify each

other" (D&C 43:8). The elders should conduct these meetings according to the promptings of the Holy Ghost. (D&C
20:45; 46:2.)

Verse 76's direction that the elder or priest administering
the sacrament should "kneel with the church" does not necessarily mean that the congregation must also be kneeling.

Thoughtfully comparing the sacrament prayers in verses 77
and 79 with the requirements for membership set forth in
verse 37 shows how directly the sacrament is a renewal of
specific covenants made at baptism. A later revelation (D&C
27:2–4) instructed that it is not necessary to use wine for the
sacrament. Bread and water have become the customary emblems, but these are not specifically required by the scriptures.

Section 21: The Lord Acknowledges His Church

Because the Church was organized "agreeable to the laws
of our country" (D&C 20:1), at least six initial members
were required. They were Joseph, Hyrum, and Samuel
Smith, Oliver Cowdery, Peter Whitmer, Jr., and David Whitmer. The following is a brief summary of what was done at
this momentous meeting held on *Tuesday*, April 6, 1830:

1. The meeting was opened by solemn prayer.
2. Those present voted unanimously to organize the
Church and to accept Joseph Smith and Oliver Cowdery as
"their teachers in the things of the kingdom of God."
3. Joseph and Oliver ordained one another elders.
4. The sacrament was administered and passed.
5. Each member present was confirmed by the laying on of
hands, and the Holy Ghost was poured out "to a very great
degree."
6. Section 21 was received during the meeting.
7. Others were ordained to various priesthood offices.
8. Following inspired testimony bearing, the meeting was
closed. (*HC*, 1:74–79.)

In this revelation the Lord accepted his newly organized
Church. Note that his very first commandment to the Church
was to keep a record. (See discussion under section 47 herein.)
Joseph Smith's titles listed in verse 1 describe various functions

of the president of the Church: A *seer* sees spiritually and is qualified to use the Urim and Thummim (Mosiah 8:13-16); *translator* focuses on Joseph's role in bringing forth ancient scriptures; a *prophet* is one who speaks for God; an *apostle* is a "special witness" for Christ (D&C 107:23); *elder* is the title of one bearing the Melchizedek Priesthood.

The Lord first addressed Joseph Smith personally (verse 1), but then admonished the whole Church to give heed to the Prophet's words "as if from mine own mouth." (Verses 4-5; compare D&C 1:38.) Finally, the Lord addressed Oliver Cowdery, whom he called to be the "first preacher" for the Church and to the world. (Verses 10-12.)

Section 22 and the Question of Rebaptism

Following the organization of the Church, those who had been baptized previously for the remission of sins were now baptized again, specifically for admission into the Church. The question answered in this revelation did not concern these persons, however, but referred to some who had been baptized only in other churches. The Lord pointed out that "the new and everlasting covenant," his gospel (D&C 66:2), had been restored. Because his Church and priesthood were again on earth, all "old covenants" or rites of other churches were done away, and therefore if a person received even a hundred baptisms performed without priesthood authority, they would avail him nothing. This revelation, in conjunction with Section 20, was acknowledged as part of the "Articles and Covenants of the Church" at the first conference held June 9, 1830. (*Far West Record,* p. 1.)

Section 23

The revelations to these five men, originally published as separate sections (see Appendix A), were received within the first week after the Church was organized. The first four men, who already had been baptized, were assured that their sins were forgiven; Joseph Knight, on the other hand, was admonished to be baptized, which he did the following June. (See discussion of section 12 for background on Joseph Knight.)

Joseph Smith, Sr., (verse 5) and Hyrum Smith (verse 3) were told that they had a duty to the Church forever because of their family. This has generally been understood to refer to the office of Patriarch to the Church, which is passed down from generation to generation within their posterity. (See Chart 6.)

Section 24

Persecution mounted during June 1830, especially in the Colesville, New York, area. Joseph Smith had to withstand violence and even arrest at the hands of his enemies. (See *HC,* 1:86–101.) This was the setting for section 24 and the following two sections. (See, for example, D&C 24:8.)

"Magnify Thine Office" (Verses 3–9). Joseph Smith was counseled to magnify his calling by devoting his full time to the work of the ministry. He was assured that the three main Church branches—Manchester, Fayette, and Colesville—would support him. (Verses 3 and 7. For a discussion of the remuneration of full-time Church officers, see p. 77.) The Prophet was further warned that his strength and prime responsibility did not lie within temporal pursuits. (Verse 9.) Verse 5 contains the first instruction to write the Lord's revelations. It was about this time that Joseph Smith began collecting and copying the revelations for possible publication.

Missionary Instructions (Verses 10–19). Missionaries were directed to shake the dust off their feet as a witness against the wicked. (See the discussion under section 75 herein.) They were to go with neither "purse nor scrip" (see explanation under section 84 herein) and were not to be concerned with such material preparation as "staves" (meaning "staffs").

Section 25 and Emma Smith

Even though this is the only section directed specifically to a woman, most of the principles and promises in the Doctrine and Covenants apply to both men and women alike. (See, for example, D&C 11:27; 12:7; and 93:49.) Emma Smith's first responsibility was to be a comfort and a true companion to her husband (verse 5); she was not to com-

Chart 6
Asael Smith and His Descendants

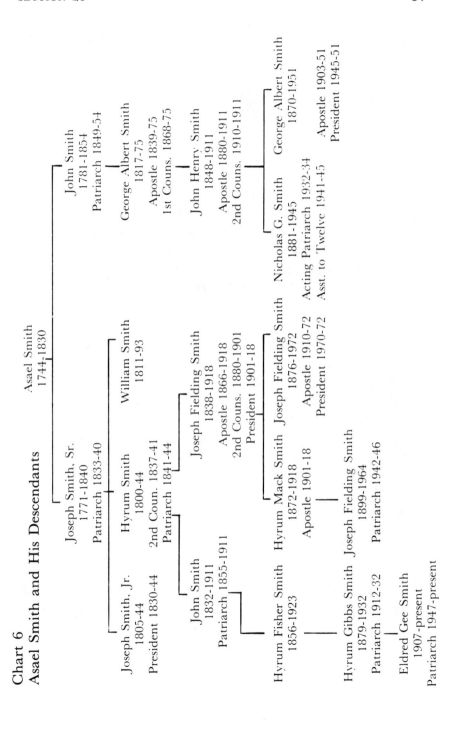

Emma Smith (Photo courtesy LDS Church archives)

plain about not having seen the Book of Mormon plates (verse 4). In addition to her major responsibility as a wife, Emma was told that she was an "elect lady" (verse 3) who would be "ordained" (meaning "set apart," the two terms being used interchangeably at the time) to teach the scriptures. (Verse 7.) When the Relief Society was organized in 1842, Joseph Smith explained that Emma had been called an elect lady because she was "elected to a certain work" and that this was fulfilled in her call as president of the new organization. (*HC* 4:552-53.) She was also to expand her talents by devoting her time "to writing, and to learning much." (Verse 8.) Emma was also directed to make a selection of hymns; her compilation was published in 1835. Verses 11 and 12 suggest the true purpose of hymns in our worship.

Section 26

Section 26 gives the name "common consent" to the important privilege of voting to sustain Church officers. (See the discussion of D&C 20:65 herein.)

Section 27

The first four verses record the personal message of an angel who gave the Prophet instructions concerning sacramental emblems. (See discussion of the sacrament under D&C 20:75-79 herein.)

Identity of Elias (Verses 6-9). The name or title *Elias* is used in the scriptures in at least three different senses:

1. *Elias* and *Elijah* are two forms of the same name, the former coming from the Greek and the latter from the Hebrew. Many references to *Elias* in the New Testament actually mean *Elijah*. For example, it was Elijah who appeared with Moses on the Mount of Transfiguration. (See Matthew 17:1-3.) Joseph Smith used the two forms of this name in his discussion of the powers of the Aaronic Priesthood and Melchizedek Priesthood respectively. (*Teachings*, pp. 335-41.)

2. *Elias* is the title of a messenger or forerunner. Perhaps John the Baptist is the best known of those who have come in the spirit of Elias.

3. There was a great prophet who lived in the days of Abraham who was particularly known as *Elias.* This prophet appeared in the Kirtland Temple in 1836 and restored the "dispensation of the gospel of Abraham." (D&C 110:12.) Joseph Fielding Smith taught that this great prophet was none other than Noah; Doctrine and Covenants 27:7 states that Elias visited Zacharias; Luke 1:19 identifies the visitor as the angel Gabriel—or Noah, who stood next to Adam in holding the keys (*Teachings,* p. 157.)

One must decide from the context which of these meanings of *Elias* is intended in each reference.

Identity of Michael (Verse 11). The great personality known as *Michael* or *the Ancient of Days* is Adam.

Section 28

Who May Receive Revelation? (Verses 1-7). Hiram Page, one of the Eight Witnesses to the Book of Mormon, claimed to be receiving revelation for the Church by means of a special stone in his possession. For example, he professed to have been told where the future city of Zion was to be built. This, of course, was contrary to the pattern set forth in the revelation given at the organization of the Church (D&C 21:1-9) that the Lord would speak to the Church through his prophet, Joseph Smith. The Prophet had at first thought of bringing this problem before the conference scheduled for September 26; but when he learned that the Whitmer family and even Oliver Cowdery were being influenced by Page's claims, he knew the matter could not wait, so he went to the Lord in prayer and received section 28 in response.

The Lord directed Oliver Cowdery to tell Hiram Page in private that his supposed revelations were not of God. Oliver would probably have had more influence with Page than would Joseph Smith because Oliver had believed in the false revelations. A close personal relationship existed among Hiram Page, Oliver Cowdery, and the Whitmers; in 1825, Page had married Katherine Whitmer, and Cowdery would marry Elizabeth Ann Whitmer in 1832.

In section 28, verses 1-7, the Lord clearly informed Oliver

that he should preach and teach as guided by the Spirit, but that it was not his privilege to receive formal revelations or commandments for the Church. Similarly, today all members of the Church are entitled to receive answers to their prayers and to have revelation to guide them in their personal affairs, family responsibilities, or Church assignments; still, only one, the President of the Church, is authorized to speak for the Lord to the Church or to the world as a whole.

A similar problem also brought forth section 43. In verses 1–7 the Lord explained that only the Prophet would receive revelation for the Church, so that all may be done in order and "that you may not be deceived." Doctrine and Covenants 43:4 states that no one else would be appointed to this responsibility except through the Prophet, and that if his calling were taken from him, he would only have authority to name his successor. This last provision would effectively silence any false prophet who obviously could not show that Joseph Smith had passed his authority on to him. The Lord knew, furthermore, that Joseph Smith would remain faithful so that his calling would not be taken from him.

Mission to the Lamanites (Verse 8). Oliver Cowdery was called to "go unto the Lamanites." (D&C 30:5–8.) Peter Whitmer, Jr., Parley P. Pratt, and Ziba Peterson were soon called to the same work. (D&C 30:5–6; 32:1–4.) These missionaries left Fayette late in October 1830. They first visited the Catteraugus Indians near Buffalo, where they left copies of the Book of Mormon. Thus the first formal mission of the Church carried the message of the restored gospel to the Lamanites and gave them the record of their fathers. (See discussion under section 3 herein, "Who Are the Lamanites?") In Church history, however, the major significance of this mission was not in its work with the Indians. Parley P. Pratt wanted to take the Book of Mormon to his old friend Sidney Rigdon, who was a leading minister at Mentor (near Kirtland), Ohio, in the Campbellite movement, a forerunner of the Disciples of Christ church. As a result of this visit, many future Church leaders were converted, including Rigdon (section 35 was later directed to him), Edward Partridge (sections 36 and 41), and Frederick G. Williams (section 81). By the following spring, there were about 1,000 members of the Church in the area. In the meantime the missionaries continued their journey west during the winter of 1830–31. Because of sectarian jealousy, the Latter-day Saint missionaries were expelled from among the Indians west of the Missouri River, but they were successful in converting many non-Indians in the vicinity of Independence, Missouri. By the spring of 1831, therefore, there were sizable Church congregations in Kirtland, Ohio, and Independence, Missouri—two centers which would play key roles in subsequent Church history.

Section 29

This is one of the great doctrinal revelations in the Doctrine and Covenants. Verses 1–30 deal mostly with events of the future. Verses 30–50 deal with a variety of topics ranging from pre-existence and creation to the status of little children. All this helped the members of the Church gain perspective and understanding during the early months of its existence. (Doxey, *The Doctrine and Covenants Speaks,* chapters 19 and 20 present a very good discussion of this significant section.)

Warning of Future Perils (Verses 3–30). The early Saints were warned to repent of their sins and to gather together as a protection against the latter-day tribulations. (Verses 3–8.) The Lord outlined the calamities which would befall the wicked both before and following the Millennium. The Twelve who will assist in judging Israel (verse 12) will include Matthias rather than Judas. (For a further consideration of latter-day events, see the discussion of section 45 herein.)

"Spiritual and Temporal" (Verses 31–34). The word *temporal* may have a double meaning as it is used here. First, it is used to refer to that which is material in contrast to that which is spiritual. Second, it and the word *temporary* come from the same root and have a similar meaning. The Lord declared that the "beginning of my work" was "first spiri-

tual, secondly temporal." (Verses 31-32.) For example, the earth was created spiritually and later physically. (Moses 3:5-7.) Similarly, each individual lived as a spirit son or daughter of God before receiving a physical body at the time of mortal birth. The Lord then indicated that "the last of my work" will be "first temporal, and secondly spiritual." (Verse 32.) Eventually this earth will be quickened to become a celestial world; although it will still be physical, it will be spiritual in character. (See Chart 10, p. 122.) In a like manner, the individual's resurrected body will be tangible and spiritual, being quickened by spirit rather than by blood. Hence, that which is spiritual is more enduring and therefore more vital.

Satan and the Preearthly Existence (Verses 36-39). Section 29 clarifies the biblical reference to a war in heaven (Revelation 12:4, 7-9) and indicates definitely that the spirit children of God enjoyed free agency in his presence and that Satan was successful in leading away one-third of all the spirits. Satan and his followers were cast out because—
1. they rebelled against God,
2. Satan would destroy man's agency, and
3. Satan wanted God's glory. (See Moses 4:3. Read also Moses 4:1-4 and Abraham 3:19-28 for additional information about the council in heaven which led up to these events.)

The Fall of Adam (Verses 39-45). These verses, along with 2 Nephi 2:15-27 and Moses 5:10-11, are the major source of information about the consequences of Adam's transgression, which are summarized in Chart 7. One can appreciate the need for and the accomplishments of the Atonement best by first gaining an understanding of the background of Adam's transgression. On the chart, a plus mark is placed next to each entry representing a condition which would be considered favorable if it were a quality of one's eternal state; a minus indicates those qualities which would be regarded as undesirable. It can be seen that Adam's transgression brought a "fall" in at least three areas:
1. He became mortal.

2. Adam and Eve were cast out of the Lord's presence and became spiritually dead because of their disobedience.

3. They fell from a terrestrial to a telestial level.

Keep in mind that the second column represents our present state. Because of our own sins, we have brought upon ourselves spiritual death—not that our spirit dies, but that our unworthiness impairs our ability to receive the blessings of spiritual life. Further reflection will suggest that the Fall was really just a step down along the path which leads to eternal life; being outside of God's immediate presence, subject to the limitations of mortality and in a telestial state in which Satan's influence is near, gives the individual the opportunities necessary in preparing for eternal life and exaltation through adhering to the gospel. (See D&C 122:5-7.) It is interesting to note that all the favorable aspects of Adam and Eve's condition before their transgression, as well as of our present condition, will be enjoyed by the faithful through the atonement of Jesus Christ.

Chart 7

Consequences of Adam's Transgression

Adam and Eve before Fall	After Fall (Our present condition)	Available through Atonement
+Not mortal	−Mortal: subject to physical death	+Immortal: resurrection
+Presence of God	−Cast out: spiritual death	+May return to presence of God through obedience
−No knowledge of good and evil	+Knowledge	+Knowledge
−No posterity	+Have children	+Eternal increase
−Terrestrial	−Telestial	+Celestial

Little Children (Verses 46-48). There is a distinction between *sin* and *transgression.* Sin is usually used to refer to a willful, deliberate, knowing transgression of God's law. Little children lack the knowledge necessary to *sin.* Satan is not given the power to tempt them. One of the most vigorous denunciations of the doctrine that children are sinful and, therefore, need baptism is found in the writings of the ancient prophet Mormon. He said that such a doctrine is a "solemn mockery before God" and that he who teaches it "is in the gall of bitterness and in the bonds of iniquity" because he is making our Father a partial God by denying his mercy and by setting "at naught the atonement." (Moroni 8:8–9, 14, 20.)

The Lord returned to the theme of parents' responsibility to their children in Doctrine and Covenants 68:25–28 and indicated that eight years was the age for baptism. Children do not become wholly responsible at once, and the Lord will hold a person accountable only in proportion to his responsibility. But in order to avoid confusion, the Lord has indicated that he will hold no one accountable before the age of eight years, at which time the child should be baptized.

Those who die before the age of accountability will not be deprived of any blessing they might have received had they lived to maturity in the flesh, but they will be given the opportunity to earn their exaltation in the celestial kingdom. (See Joseph F. Smith, *Gospel Doctrine*, p. 453, and Joseph Fielding Smith, *Answers to Gospel Questions*, Vol. 1, pp. 57–59.)

State of the Mentally Retarded. (Verses 49–50). These verses suggest that those who have "no understanding," like little children, are not capable of sin, so need no baptism.

Sections 30–36

Sections 30 and 32 added three men to the Lamanite mission, while more brethren were being called to several other fields of labor. To prepare the world for the Lord's second coming, these missionaries were to preach the gospel, which is defined succinctly in D&C 33:10–12 and 39:6.

A sense of urgency was given to the missionaries' assignment as the Lord used such phrases as: "Reap in the field which is white already to be *burned*." "It is the eleventh hour, and the last time that I shall call laborers into my vineyard." "Even now already summer is nigh." (D&C 31:4; 33:3; 35:16.) Note that sections 33–35 end with the warning, "I come quickly."

Sidney Rigdon (Photo courtesy Harold B. Lee Library)

Several future Church leaders were addressed in these revelations. Thomas B. Marsh (section 31) became the original
President of the Twelve in 1835; he failed to heed the counsel given him in verses 9 and 12, so ultimately lost his high
standing. Parley P. Pratt (section 32) and his younger brother Orson (section 34) were both members of the original
Quorum of the Twelve. Even though Orson Pratt was only
nineteen years old when he received section 34, he was told
that he would preach "as with the sound of a trump, both
long and loud" (verse 6); this prophecy was fulfilled in Elder
Pratt's lifetime of missionary service. Sidney Rigdon (section
35) later served as first counselor in the First Presidency. (See
discussion below.) Edward Partridge, who became the first
Presiding Bishop, was not yet a member when he received
section 36. The last two of these brethren first heard the gospel in Ohio from the missionaries to the Lamanites. (See the
discussion of this mission under section 28 herein.) Shortly afterward they journeyed from Kirtland to Fayette in order to
meet the Prophet personally. This was the setting for sections
35 and 36.

Sidney Rigdon's "Greater Work" (D&C 35:3–6). Some Latter-day Saints take the view that there is no good at all being done by other churches. Apparently the Lord regarded Sidney Rigdon's service as a Campbellite minister as a *great* work because he described it as preparation for a *greater* work. Without knowing it, Sidney had prepared his congregation to receive the restored gospel. Verse 4 suggests he had labored in the same spirit as John the Baptist, who was sent to prepare the way for the coming of the Savior. Still it was necessary for Sidney Rigdon and his followers to join the only true Church. The contrast between his past work and his future opportunities was suggested in verses 5–6, the words in brackets being inserted to sharpen the meaning:

[*Without priesthood authority*] *thou didst baptize by water unto repentance, but they received not the Holy Ghost;*

But now I give unto thee a commandment, that thou shalt baptize by water [*having the authority*], *and* [*therefore*] *they shall receive the Holy Ghost by the laying on of hands, even as the apostles of old.*

The Lord gave a similar message to James Covill, who had been a Baptist minister for about forty years. In section 39, verses 10–12, he was commanded to be baptized and was promised that he, too, could do a "greater work"—preach the fullness of the restored gospel with power.

In section 35, Sidney Rigdon received two specific assignments to work with Joseph Smith:

1. He was to act as scribe for the Prophet, who would have the scriptures unfolded to him by the Lord's power (verse 20); this may be a reference to the inspired revision of the Bible.

2. Sidney was to use his training as a minister to prove from the scriptures the truth of the words Joseph Smith would receive through revelation; this relationship between Joseph and Sidney was reiterated in Doctrine and Covenants 100:9–11.

The Inspired Revision of the Bible. Statements about the Prophet "translating" the scriptures during this period often referred to his inspired revision of the Bible. This was not a "translation" in the usual sense of the word because no foreign language texts were involved. The Prophet received through revelation revisions which clarified the meaning of the King James Version. Still, the Inspired Version is more than merely commentary on the meaning of biblical passages; it appears in many instances to be a restoration of the original, or, strictly speaking, an inspired English translation of the original Hebrew, Aramaic, and Greek writings. In this latter sense, the Inspired Version might be called a "translation."

This project may have begun when the Prophet received the book of Moses by revelation during June and December 1830. By September of that year he had started his work of revising the Old Testament. In the following March, the Lord directed the Prophet to work on the New Testament. (See D&C 45:60–61.) He completed this phase of the project by February 2, 1833. Roughly a month later, the Lord spoke to the Prophet about finishing "the translation of the prophets," that is, the Old Testament (D&C 90:13), and also counseled him not to revise the Apocrypha. (See section 91.) On July 2, 1833, Joseph Smith recorded: "We this day finished the translating of the Scriptures, for which we returned gratitude to our Heavenly Father." (*HC,* 1:368.)

The revisions in the Inspired Version help clarify biblical passages and gospel doctrines. These changes are most numerous in the books of Genesis and Matthew. Because the revisions were given by inspiration, this version is a most valuable work to study.

Joseph Smith's "new translation" of the Bible has contributed to our knowledge of gospel doctrines in still another way. Questions which arose in relation to biblical passages became the occasions for the Prophet's receiving many revelations now in the Doctrine and Covenants. Some of these include sections 74, 76, 77, 86, 91, 93, 113, and 132. Nevertheless, The Church of Jesus Christ of Latter-day Saints has not adopted the Inspired Version as one of its standard works because the Prophet never considered the project really completed, even though he had "finished" in the sense that he had gone all the way through the Bible. Joseph Smith's revision has been published by the Reorganized Church under the title The Holy Scriptures.

(For an excellent discussion, see Robert J. Matthews, *"A Plainer Translation": Joseph Smith's Translation of the Bible, A History and Commentary* [Provo: BYU Press, 1975].)

Sections 37-38 and the Move to Ohio

Both sections 37 and 38 deal with the Lord's command that the Church should move to "the Ohio" country. It will be remembered that through the efforts of the missionaries to the Lamanites, there was already a growing center of Church membership in and around Kirtland, Ohio, near the shores of Lake Erie. (See discussion of the Lamanite mission under section 28 herein.) This was the beginning of the westward movement which was to be so important a theme in Church history for several decades to come.

The Place of Jesus Christ (D&C 38:1-4). The Lord's exalted station is reflected in various titles applied to him. "I Am" suggests that he is the source of all being. "Alpha and Omega," the first and last letters of the Greek alphabet, suggest that all is encompassed within his power. He is the creator of the world, the Jehovah of the Old Testament. By virtue of his atonement, he is able to be our "advocate" who pleads our cause before the Father. (Compare verse 4 with D&C 45:3-5.)

1831, A Significant Year. Section 37 was the last recorded revelation received in 1830, and section 38 was the first received in 1831—the year during which more recorded revelations were received than during any other. These include sections 38-72, as well as sections 1 and 133, and explain many basic doctrines.

Sections 39-40 and James Covill

Although Covill had been a Baptist preacher for forty years, he was now commanded to be baptized by priesthood authority. (Compare section 39, verse 10, with section 22.) Like Sidney Rigdon, he was prepared for a "greater work"—to preach the *fulness* of the gospel. (Verse 11.) Nevertheless, the

Lord warned him against pride (verse 9), and instructed him not to go east where he might attract the world's recognition, but rather to go to Ohio with the Saints (verse 14).

Despite good intentions, Covill failed to follow the Lord's counsel. Section 40, explaining Covill's failure, was given to Sidney Rigdon, another former minister who might face similar temptations.

Section 41 and the Arrival in Kirtland

In obedience to the commandment in sections 37 and 38, Joseph Smith led the way in the Saints' move to Ohio, arriving in Kirtland on February 1, 1831. He found the people organized into "families" or communal units in which all private property was turned over to the group according to the system of "common stock." Some curious deviations had crept into these people's attempt to revive New Testament Christianity. The Lord instructed the elders of his Church to come together in faith and he would give them the correct law by which they were to live (verses 2–3); this promise was fulfilled five days later with the giving of section 42, commonly known as "the law of the Church." The calling of a bishop was essential to the operation of the new law. Note how Edward Partridge's appointment as the first bishop in the Church included three essential steps: (1) a call by the Lord; (2) sustaining by the "voice of the Church"; and (3) ordination by proper authority. (See verse 9.)

Section 42: The Law of the Church

The Lord's law contained in this section was given in fulfillment of the promise in Doctrine and Covenants 38:32 and according to the Lord's arrangement made in 41:2–3. Section 42 is actually composed of three revelations. Verses 1–72 were received February 9, 1831. Verses 74–77 and 78–93 were received February 23. The words "high priests" in verses 31 and 71 and "high council" in verse 34 were added in the 1835 edition after these offices were restored. Section 42 contains a series of laws:

1. Law concerning preaching the gospel. (Verses 4–17.)

Edward Partridge (Photo courtesy Harold B. Lee Library)

2. Law of moral commandments. (Verses 18–29.)
3. Law of consecration. (Verses 30–42.)
4. Administering to the sick. (Verses 43–52.)
5. Law of remuneration. (Verses 70–73.)
6. Punishment for transgression. (Verses 74–93.)

Teaching the Gospel (Verses 4-17)

Compliance with these instructions is vital to success in the Lord's work. Missionaries' going "two by two" (verse 6) not only affords necessary protection but also provides the essential second witness for what is taught. Requiring recognized authority (verse 11) helps weed out false pretenders from the Lord's work. Teachers should center their instruction in the scriptures (compare verse 12 with D&C 52:9); the "fulness of my scriptures" (verse 15) refers to Joseph Smith's inspired revision of the Bible. (See the discussion under sections 30 and 31 herein.) All were to follow approved Church procedures.

(Verse 13; for a discussion of the "covenants and church articles," see p. 5.) Finally, one cannot teach the gospel effectively unless he has the power of the Holy Ghost. (Compare
verse 14 with 2 Nephi 33:1.)

Moral Commandments

Commandments Reviewed (Verses 18–29). In these verses the
Lord reviewed some of the Ten Commandments. While verse
23 and also Doctrine and Covenants 63:16 list some of the
negative fruits of immorality, section 42:22 suggests a positive
reason for chastity—that one may save his full love for that
person whom he hopes he can make his eternal companion.
For a discussion as to why murder and adultery under certain conditions cannot be forgiven, see the description of unpardonable and unforgivable sins under Sections 19 and 132
herein.)

Fornication vs. Adultery (Verses 74–77). The First Presidency has
declared: "The Lord has drawn no essential distinctions between fornication, adultery, and harlotry or prostitution.
Each has fallen under His solemn and awful condemnation."
(*CR*, October 1942, p. 11.) Therefore, the distinction made in
verses 74–75 appears not to be between fornication and adultery as much as it is between those who are personally guilty
or innocent of the offense. Verses 76–77 suggest that sexual
immorality is a more serious transgression for married than
for single individuals; a married person who sins is not only
committing the immoral act, but is also breaking the covenant of fidelity made at marriage.

Confession of Sins (Verses 88–92). In answer to the question
"To whom are we to confess our sins?", Elder Marion G.
Romney concluded: "I would assume that we are to confess
all our sins unto the Lord. For transgressions which are
wholly personal, affecting none but ourselves and the Lord,
such confession would seem to be sufficient. For misconduct
which offends another, confession should also be made to the
offended one, and forgiveness sought." (*CR*, October 1955, p.
125.) In section 42 the Lord emphasized that such confession

need be no more public than was the offense. Elder Romney continued: "Finally where one's transgressions are of such a nature as would, unrepented of, put in jeopardy his right to membership or fellowship in the Church of Jesus Christ, full and effective confession would, in my judgment, require confession by the repentant sinner to his bishop or other proper presiding Church officer—not that the Church officer would forgive the sin . . . but rather that the Church, acting through its duly appointed officers, might with full knowledge of the facts take such action with respect to Church discipline as the circumstances merit." (Ibid.)

The Law of Consecration (Verses 30–42)

This law was an important part of the restoration of all things. In addition, it was given to acquaint the Saints with what will be expected if they are to build Zion. Furthermore, the Lord had commanded his people to be one (D&C 38:27), for, as he subsequently explained, "if ye are not equal in earthly things ye cannot be equal in obtaining heavenly things" (D&C 78:6).

Functioning of the Law. An individual who recognized that everything on this earth was really the Lord's (Psalm 24:1) and who had the desire to build the kingdom of God would *consecrate* all his property to the Lord's authorized representative, the bishop. This was done by formal legal deed, transferring title of all property from the individual to the bishop. (Verses 30–32.) This property was placed in the bishop's storehouse from which he also drew the property that was to become the consecrator's *stewardship,* also called his *inheritance* or *portion.* This stewardship was to be based not only on the individual or his family's needs, but also on their "circumstances" (including abilities, talents, etc.) and on their "just wants." (See D&C 51:3 and 82:17.) Joseph Smith instructed the bishop not to accept an individual's consecration unless both parties could agree on the size and nature of the stewardship. Even though everyone thought of this property as being the Lord's, the stewardship was nevertheless given to the individual by formal deed; thus, even if he left the

Church, the individual would retain title to his stewardship. (See D&C 51:4–5.) Therefore, he could not claim his original consecration. (See D&C 42:37.) The individual then felt not only the usual economic pressures, but also a religious or spiritual obligation to develop or *magnify his stewardship.* That which he produced above his family's needs or wants was designated a *surplus* and was transferred to the bishop's storehouse. (See verse 55.) From this source, as well as from the *residue* which would result from an excess of consecration over property needed for original assignment of stewardships, the bishop could help the poor, buy land, erect Church buildings, and establish Zion on earth. (See verses 34–35.) In addition, this property could be used to expand the existing stewardships of all in the order or to improve community conditions; thus, there would be an economic profit motive of a sort, but rather than being on a purely selfish basis, it would be broadened to include the well-being of the whole group.

The Law of Consecration Today. Elder Henry D. Taylor pointed out that from its beginning the Church has—

1. encouraged members to establish and maintain their economic independence,

2. encouraged habits of thrift and the avoiding of debt,

3. fostered the establishment of employment-creating industries, and

4. stood ready at all times to help needy, faithful members. ("The Principles of the Welfare Plan," *BYU Speeches of the Year,* May 16, 1962, p. 2.)

These principles were part of the law of consecration during the 1830s as well as of the Welfare Program of the 1930s. President J. Reuben Clark, Jr., declared: "We have all said that the Welfare Plan is not the United Order and was not intended to be. However, I should like to suggest to you that perhaps, after all, when the Welfare Plan gets thoroughly into operation . . . we shall not be so very far from carrying out the great fundamentals of the United Order." (*CR,* October 1942, p. 57.) Elder Albert E. Bowen concurred: "It is not asserted that the Welfare Plan is the United Order, but perhaps there is a much greater nearness of approach than we have been accustomed to think. Safe it is to say that a complete living of the law governing this plan, and the practice of the principles involved, would make the transition into the organization of the United Order not too difficult." (Albert E. Bowen, *The Church Welfare Plan* [Salt Lake City: Deseret Sunday School Union, 1946], p. 145.)

Fundamental similarities exist between the law of consecration and the tithing, fast offering, and welfare programs of the Church. Elder Marion G. Romney explained that tithing "implements to a degree at least the United Order principle of stewardships, for it leaves in the hands of each person the ownership and management of the property for which he produces the needs of himself and family." In place of the *residues* and *surpluses* of the law of consecration today,

Chart 8

How the Law of Consecration Works

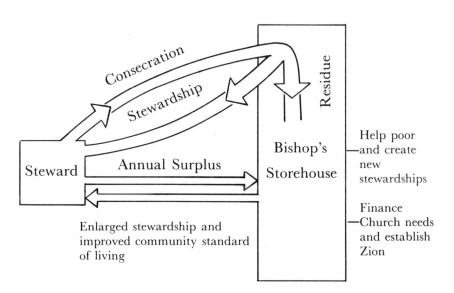

Church members contribute tithes, fast offerings, and other donations to be used for similar purposes—aiding those in need and building the Church for the kingdom of God on earth. The bishops storehouse is a key institution, and during the twentieth century it fulfills a function similar to its function under the law of consecration. Elder Romney concluded:

We as bearers of the priesthood should live strictly by the principles of the United Order, insofar as they are embodied in present Church practices, such as the fast offering, tithing, and the welfare activities. Through these practices we could as individuals, if we were of a mind to do so, implement in our lives all the basic principles of the United Order. (Marion G. Romney, "Socialism and the United Order Compared," Improvement Era, June 1966, p. 537.)

Consecration vs. Communism. Some have confused the ideals of the law of consecration with communism as practiced in the Soviet Union. Elder Marion G. Romney says that even though both "deal with the production and distribution of goods" and seek the temporal well-being of mankind by eliminating economic inequalities and selfishness, there are still fundamental differences, including the following:

1. "The cornerstone of the United Order is belief in God and acceptance of Him as Lord of the earth and the Author of the United Order. Socialism, wholly materialistic, is founded in the wisdom of men and not of God. Although all socialists may not be atheists, none of them in theory or practice seek the Lord to establish His righteousness."

2. The United Order preserved free agency and was implemented by voluntary consecrations, while socialism depends on external state power.

3. Unlike socialism, the law of consecration further recognized free agency by preserving the principles of "private ownership and individual management." (Ibid.)

Blessing the Sick (Verses 43–52)

We must not overlook the power of faith, of the Holy Ghost, and of the priesthood in healing the sick. Compare the instructions in verse 44 with James 5:14. Even those with faith to be healed should do all possible to preserve or restore their health through obtaining proper care; this parallels the Lord's instruction that we seek answers through our own efforts as well as through asking him. (Compare D&C 9:7-9.)

The righteous are not promised that they will never die. Reading verses 46-47 carefully shows that they will not "taste of death"—meaning that death will hold no fear for them.

God has appointed the time when we enter and leave this mortal sphere. (Verse 48.) We may hasten the time of our death through carelessness, but we probably cannot delay it much. (For an excellent discussion of this subject, see Spencer W. Kimball, "Tragedy or Destiny," in *Faith Precedes the Miracle* [Salt Lake City: Deseret Book, 1972], pp. 95-106; see also Doxey, *The Doctrine and Covenants Speaks,* chap. 29.)

Remuneration for Church Service (Verses 70-73)

In section 24 the Lord had told Joseph Smith to magnify his office by devoting his full time to the Church, that his strength lay in spiritual rather than in temporal things, and that it was the duty of these churches to support him. (See D&C 24:3, 7, 9.) The Lord later directed the Church to build a house for the Prophet. (D&C 41:7.) In section 43, those who wanted to know the glorious mysteries of the gospel were told to uphold other temporal necessities. (See D&C 43:12-13.) Thus, Latter-day Saints believe that anyone who is called to devote his full time to the Church should receive his full support from the Church. There are at least two major differences between this practice in the restored Church and the "paid ministry" in the churches of the world:

1. A Latter-day Saint cannot elect to enter the ministry as a vocation to earn his living; one assumes Church assignments only upon a call through those in authority.

2. In contrast to the patterns common in most denominations in which a full-time professional clergy is the rule, among the Latter-day Saints relatively very few (such as the General Authorities, mission presidents, etc.) are asked to devote full time to Church work. Instead, the majority are giv-

en the opportunity of giving part of their time, and, thus, many share in the blessings of Church service.

Section 42 relates the principle of remuneration for full-time service to the law of consecration. (See verses 70-73.) For such individuals, their Church assignment is their stewardship, the magnifying of which should qualify them to receive support as would be true with an ordinary stewardship. Similarly, the Lord appointed those who had worked with the publication of the compiled revelations to be stewards over the project and to derive their temporal support therefrom. (See D&C 70:1-7.) In that same revelation, the Lord explained that even though those who administer spiritual things may receive an abundance through the Spirit, they should be equal in temporal things with those whose stewardship is temporal. (See verses 12-14.)

Section 43

When a woman named Hubble professed to have received the Lord's law for the Church by revelation, this was a direct challenge to the authority of Joseph Smith, through whom God had just given "the law of the Church" (section 42.) Hiram Page's earlier claim to revelation had brought forth a similar message from the Lord upholding the position of his prophet. (See the discussion of section 28 herein.)

In section 43, the elders were admonished to uphold Joseph Smith (verses 12-13) and were reminded that their responsibility was to teach what they received through revelation rather than be taught by other men. They were to warn the nations to prepare for that which is to come. (See discussion of section 45 herein.)

Section 44

In accordance with the Lord's direction in this revelation, the elders held their conference at Kirtland early in the following June. The Lord's promise to pour out his Spirit (verse 2) was fulfilled on that occasion. (See discussion under section 52 herein.)

Section 45: The Signs of the Times

When the Church was almost a year old, the spreading of

the gospel message was hampered greatly by many false stories which aroused prejudice against the Latter-day Saints. For example, many newspapers in the area carried the story of a Mormon girl predicting an earthquake in China which caused great destruction just six weeks later. These papers labeled the loss of thousands of lives in that disaster as being " 'Mormonism' in China." (*HC*, 1:58). This section contains a valid revelation from the Lord describing that which is to come.

The revelation is an outstanding example of the benefits flowing from Joseph Smith's "new translation" of the Bible. During the spring of 1831 the Prophet was working on his inspired revision of Matthew, including chapter 24 in which the Savior instructed his disciples concerning the last days. Beginning in verse 16 of section 45 the Lord repeated and amplified many of these teachings and applied them to the circumstances of his Latter-day Saints. Hence "this place" (verse 43) refers to the Holy Land, and "this mount" (verse 48) designates the Mount of Olives. The Lord promised that more concerning "this chapter" (verse 60) would be made known through the Prophet's "translation" of the New Testament; the inspired revision of Matthew 24 is now found in the Pearl of Great Price.

The Lord warned in this revelation that those who fear him will be looking for the signs of his coming. (See verses 39-40.) He has also promised that to the faithful "it shall be given to know the signs of the times, and the signs of the coming of the Son of Man." (D&C 68:11.)

Because the Doctrine and Covenants is a "voice of warning" (D&C 1:4), a discussion of signs of things to come is an important theme running throughout the entire book. The following are only some of the revelations treating this subject: D&C 1:11-16, 34-36; 29:1-30; 43:17-35; 88:87-117; 101:24-34; section 133. We should base our understanding of latter-day developments on such revealed authoritative sources.

The Lord has not revealed the precise time of his coming. (Compare Matthew 24:36 with D&C 49:7.) We should rather emphasize how best to be prepared for that which is to come. (See Matthew 24:42–44 and D&C 1:12.) Latter-day events can be grouped for greater understanding as follows:

1. The "times of the Gentiles."
2. Developments following the "times of the Gentiles."
3. Events accompanying Christ's Second Advent.
4. Conditions and activities during the Millennium.
5. Events following the Millennium.

Most of these developments are outlined in section 45.

The "Times of the Gentiles" (Verses 28–30). This period would "come in" or begin with the restoration of the gospel (verse 28), which would first be given to the gentiles. (D&C 90:9; 107:33–34.) Prophecies in the Book of Mormon differentiate "gentiles" from other groups such as the Lamanites, Jews, and heathens. President Marion G. Romney defined *gentiles* as "the present inhabitants of America" and "the people of the Old World from which they came." (*CR,* Oct. 1975, p. 54.) For a century and a quarter, Latter-day Saint missionaries had the greatest success among these groups. The time was to come, however, when these people would no longer be as receptive to the gospel, and thus the "times of the Gentiles" would be "fulfilled." (Verse 30.)

The Gathering of Israel (Verses 25, 43). The Lord warned his ancient disciples that the temple in Jerusalem would be destroyed and that the Jews would be scattered (verses 18–24), but he promised that following the "times of the Gentiles" they would be gathered again (verses 25, 43). Joseph Smith declared: "Judah must return, Jerusalem must be rebuilt, and the temple, and water come out from under the temple, and the waters of the Dead Sea be healed. It will take some time to rebuild the walls of the city and the temple, etc.; and all this must be done before the Son of Man will make His appearance." (*HC,* 5:337.) Not only the Jews but all the seed of Israel would be gathered from the nations of the earth. Moses restored the keys for this gathering in 1836. (See the discussion of D&C 110:11 herein.) Because the Lamanites will receive rich blessings, this period is often called "the day of the Lamanites."

Calamities (Verses 26–27, 31–42). A second development to follow the "times of the Gentiles" is an increase in both man-made and natural calamities. War would be poured out. (Compare verse 26 with D&C 1:35 and section 87.) Hatred and wickedness would abound. (Compare verse 27 with Joseph Smith's revision of Matthew 24 in the Pearl of Great Price, verses 7–8; for prophecies that "the Constitution will hang as a thread," see *Ensign,* June 1976, pp. 64–65.) Other D&C sections give more detail concerning awesome natural events. (Compare verses 31, 33, and 41–42 with D&C 88:87–94 and 133:22–34.) These calamities will come because of wickedness (D&C 29:14–21) and as a means to call the world to repentance (D&C 43:21, 25.) Furthermore, declared Joseph Smith, they will help clear the way for establishing Zion and the return of the Ten Tribes. (*HC* 1:315.)

The Saints' Reaction (Verses 32, 35). Even though the Lord spoke of calamities and tribulations increasing as the time of his coming draws near, he has encouraged the faithful to "stand in holy places" (verse 32; compare D&C 87:8) and be not troubled, knowing that the glorious promises are about to be fulfilled (verse 35). In an earlier revelation the Lord had assured the righteous that "if ye are prepared ye shall not fear." (D&C 38:30.) The Lord has promised the Saints protection in the midst of these afflictions. (See D&C 63:32–36; 97:25.) Elder Harold B. Lee admonished Church members to look to the First Presidency for instructions as to what they should do in these difficult times. (*CR,* April 1948, p. 55.) The Saints should watch for the signs of the times so that they might be better prepared. (Concerning the parable of the fig tree, compare verses 37–38 with D&C 35:16.)

Events Associated with Christ's Second Coming (Verses 44–55). Doctrine and Covenants 88:96–110 gives more details concerning the resurrections and judgments to accompany the Second Advent. The Lord's appearance on the Mount of Olives (verses 48–53 and Zechariah 14:2–5) is only one of several appearances he will make. (For more detail concerning his appearance to the world as a whole, see D&C 133:41–48.) Information concerning developments during and following the Millennium is found in D&C 88:110–116 and 101:24–34.

Parable of the Ten Virgins (Verses 56–59). Read this parable in Matthew 25:1–13. Note that not everyone was waiting for the bridegroom, and that only half of those waiting were prepared. Section 45 applied the parable to the latter-days, comparing the wise virgins to those who "have received the truth, and have taken the Holy Spirit for their guide." (Verse 57.) Elder Wilford Woodruff declared:

> *The parable of the ten virgins is intended to represent the second coming of the Son of Man, the coming of the Bridegroom to meet the bride, the Church . . . and I expect that the Savior was about right when he said, in reference to the members of the Church, that five of them were wise and five were foolish; . . . if he finds one-half of those professing to be members of his Church prepared for salvation, it will be as many as can be expected, judging by the course that many are pursuing. (JD, 18:110.)*

Zion (Verses 64–71). Compare the description of the latter-day Zion in these verses with the characteristics of Enoch's people (Moses 7:13–18) and of the Nephites during their "golden age" (4 Nephi 2–3, 15–17). The precise location of Zion was revealed later in 1831. (See the discussion under section 57 herein.)

Section 46: The Gifts of the Spirit

This section is an excellent example of the Lord's revealing information far beyond the circumstances which made the revelation necessary. The practice had arisen among some to exclude unbelievers from sacrament meetings. Other members of the Church regarded this custom as wrong in light of the Lord's instructions in the Book of Mormon (3 Nephi 18:22–34) to the effect that those in need of repentance should not be forbidden but should be welcomed in sacrament meetings, since this might be a means of bringing them to repentance. The Lord settled this matter in the first seven verses of section 46 by reemphasizing the fact that no one is to be excluded from any public meetings such as the sacrament meeting. Those who conduct meetings are to proceed as "directed and guided by the Holy Spirit. (Verse 2.) In verse 7, the Lord further commanded his Saints "in all things to ask of God" and then do in holiness with prayer and thanksgiving whatsoever "the Spirit testifies unto you." This opened the way for a remarkable discussion of the gifts of the Spirit—a discussion that occupies the remainder of the revelation.

Latter-day Saints are commanded, "Seek ye earnestly the best gifts" which are given for the benefit of those who love the Lord and keep his commandments. (See verses 8–9; compare 1 Corinthians 12:31.) Furthermore, this is another safeguard against being deceived. (See verses 7–8.) It will be remembered that the Lord earlier exhorted the people to follow the Prophet as another key against deception. (See D&C 43:5–6.) If one is to seek these gifts, he has to know what they are. (See verse 10.) Not all receive the same gifts, but "to some is given one, and to some is given another, that all may be profited thereby." (Verse 12.) In 1 Corinthians 12, Paul listed the various gifts of the Spirit and compared them, as well as the various officers in the Church, to a perfect human body, all of whose members are essential for the well-being of the whole. Paul's list of the gifts is similar to that found in section 46 and also Moroni 10.

It is instructive to see how the various standard works strengthen one another. For example, Paul testified that "no man can *say* that Jesus is the Christ but by the Holy Ghost" (1 Corinthians 12:3; italics added), while modern revelation suggests that "say" might better be translated "know" (D&C 46:13). The Doctrine and Covenants speaks of the "word of Wisdom" and the "word of knowledge" (D&C 46:17–18); Moroni explained that the ability to *teach* these is a gift of the Spirit (Moroni 10:9–10).

"Differences of Administration" and "Diversities of Operations" (Verses 15–16). The significance of these terms may be clarified by referring to the meaning of the Greek words which Paul used and which have been translated into English as "administration" and "operations." *Administration* describes

the various courses or duties of the priesthood. The Lord directs his authorized servants by revelation through the Holy Ghost. Knowing the *diversities of operations* means being able to discern whether or not a given form of spiritual manifestation is of the Lord. (See Sperry, *Compendium,* pp. 194–201.)

The Gift of Tongues (Verses 24–25). There are churches in the world which publicly demonstrate the ability to speak in unknown tongues as an attempt to prove they have the Holy Spirit. In contrast to this attitude, Joseph Smith pointed out that the weightier gifts, such as faith and wisdom, are not necessarily accompanied by visible outward manifestations. He also described the gift of tongues as the smallest of the gifts, its "ultimate destiny" being its power to enable one to speak with foreigners. (*HC,* 5:27–31.) In Chapter 14 of 1 Corinthians, Paul discussed some of the abuses of the gift of tongues. Even though the apostle was proud of the fact that he could speak in tongues as much as anyone in the Church, he would rather speak five words that could be understood than to speak ten thousand words in an unknown tongue. (See 1 Corinthians 14:18–19.)

Section 47 and Church History

John the Revelator declared that the dead would be judged "out of those things which were written in the books," (Revelation 20:12–13.) In commenting on this passage, the Prophet Joseph Smith warned that "whatsoever you do not record on earth shall not be recorded in heaven." (D&C 128:6–8.) Therefore record keeping has been an important part of the Lord's work from the beginning. As previously noted, the first commandment given the Church was to keep a history. (D&C 21:1.) Oliver Cowdery served as "General Church Recorder" until called to other responsibilities; section 47 then called John Whitmer to take his place. The Lord promised John Whitmer that if he was faithful he could write that which was given him by the Holy Ghost (verse 4); thus his work could be a truly unusual history and have a unique claim to certain truth. The Lord gave Elder Whitmer further instructions in section 69 concerning the history he was compiling "for the benefit of the Church and for the rising generations." (Verse 8.)

John Whitmer, unfortunately, accepted his calling reluctantly, and only after section 47 had been received. He kept a sketchy history, eighty-five manuscript pages in length. Upon his apostasy, he refused to turn his history over to the Church; only years later did it become available.

Others followed Elders Cowdery and Whitmer as "General Church Recorders." In 1838, John Corrill was called as "Church Historian," and for several years the two offices existed side by side. By 1845, Willard Richards had been called to both offices, and in October of that year he was sustained in the combined office of "Church Historian and Recorder," which continued to be held by a member of the Twelve for over a century. In 1972 the Church organized the Historical Department with two members of the Twelve as advisers and non-General Authorites serving as historian, archivist, etc. (For a discussion of the importance of record keeping, see Doxey, *The Doctrine and Covenants Speaks,* chap. 33.)

Section 48

Pursuant to the directions given in sections 37 and 38, most of the New York saints moved to Ohio during the spring of 1831. This revelation was given for their benefit, instructing them concerning the law of consecration. (See the discussion of consecration under section 42 herein.)

Section 49: The Mission to the Shakers

The Shakers, or United Society of Believers in Christ's Second Appearing, had their beginning in England during the 1700s. The main group soon came to America under the leadership of Ann Lee and flourished in the revivalist climate of the early 1800s. A large community was established in the vicinity of Kirtland, Ohio. Leman Copley was a recent convert from the Shakers, and with Sidney Rigdon and Parley P. Pratt he was called to carry the restored gospel to his former coreligionists. This mission was not very successful, at least in terms of converts baptized.

Section 49 was given to these missionaries. It sets forth

basic gospel truths and refutes specific Shaker beliefs such as the following:

1. God has two natures, male and female. In his first appearing, God came in the form of the man Jesus. "Christ's second appearing" referred to in the Shaker Church's official name, was in the form of a woman—Ann Lee. (See verse 22.)

2. Outward ordinances such as baptism by water and the laying on of hands for the gift of the Holy Ghost are unnecessary. (See verses 13–14.)

3. Although marriage was not condemned, celibacy was regarded as a higher state. (See verse 15.)

4. Shakers were vegetarians, not eating meat except in time of cold or famine. (See verses 18–21.)

Marriage is Ordained of God (Verses 15–17). Marriage is the institution ordained of God by which his spirit children who lived before the earth was formed may come here and experience the opportunity and challenge of mortality. In the great preearthly council, God said: "We will take of these materials, and we will make an earth whereon these may dwell; And we will prove them herewith, to see if they will do all things whatsoever the Lord their God shall command them." (Abraham 3:24–25.)

The Bible also teaches the importance of marriage: Genesis 2:20–24 (compare this account with Abraham 5:14–18 to see how latter-day scripture clarifies the meaning of the Bible), Mark 10:7–9, Proverbs 18:22. The apostle Peter was a married man. (See Matthew 8:14–15.) (For a consideration of Paul's teachings about marriage, see discussion of section 74 herein.) Some critics argue that Matthew 22:23–30 proves there will be no marriage in the life hereafter. The Savior did not say there would be no married people nor a state of marriage following the resurrection, but that "in the resurrection, they neither *marry,* nor are *given in marriage*" (verse 30; italics added); thus, he had reference only to the act of being married. This is in agreement with the teachings of latter-day revelation that marriages for eternity must be performed here on earth. (See D&C 132:15–16.)

Section 49:16 indicates that the principle of plural marriage had not yet been revealed to the Church.

Section 50: The Discerning of Spirits

Several waves of religious revivals swept the United States during the early years of the nineteenth century. These were characterized especially on the frontier by extreme emotional manifestations. At camp meetings, which would often last several days, the preachers' fiery sermons sometimes caused their listeners to experience such outward manifestations as "jerks," "moans," or "shouts." Elder Parley P. Pratt recorded that even among some Latter-day Saints similar physical contortions and false visions had been witnessed. The Lord gave section 50 to help the brethren know how to discern whether or not such "spiritual" manifestations were of God.

Parley P. Pratt had left a most valuable account of how this revelation (as well as several others) was received:

After we had joined in prayer in his translating room, he dictated in our presence the following revelation:—(each sentence was uttered slowly and very distinctly and with a pause between each, sufficiently long for it to be recorded, by an ordinary writer, in long hand.)

This was the manner in which all his written revelations were dictated and written. There was never any hesitation, reviewing, or reading back to keep the run of the subject, neither did any communications undergo revisions, interlinings, or corrections. As he dictated them so they stood so far as I have witnessed; and I was present to witness the dictation of several communications of several pages each. (Autobiography of Parley P. Pratt, p. 62.)

With reference to Elder Pratt's last point, note that the Prophet did make some modifications or additions when subsequent revelation expanded his understanding of doctrinal concepts or of Church organization.

The Lord gave three keys by which evil spirits might be detected:

1. Since the elders had been called to preach by the Spirit, they had the power to discern. (Compare verses 13–18 with D&C 46:23.)

2. That which is of God will edify. (Verses 22–24.)

3. Those in authority will either share in a spiritual manifestation or will be given power to rebuke it. (Verses 30–32.)

The principles set forth in section 50 should not be restricted to the discerning of false spirits only. To the contrary, verses 21–24 give the key by which Church members
can know when their leaders are speaking under the direction
of the Holy Ghost. Thus, Latter-day Saints should not only
ask the Lord to inspire those who will speak, but they should
also seek the Spirit themselves so that they might be "edified
and rejoice together."

Section 51

An earlier revelation (section 42) had given the bishop, Edward Partridge, the responsibility of administering the law of
consecration. Upon the bishop's request, the Lord gave him
more explicit instructions concerning this law. (See the discussion of consecration under section 42 herein.)

Section 52

At the conference held in Kirtland, June 3–6, 1831, the
promised outpouring of the Lord's spirit (section 44) was realized. Many prophesied. Joseph Smith learned by revelation
that John the Revelator was then among the Ten Tribes.
(See discussion under section 7 herein.) It was also on this
occasion that the first high priests in this dispensation were
ordained. Section 52 was received the day following the close
of this inspirational conference. The elders were to go two by
two to Missouri where the Lord would consecrate a land for
the gathering of Israel. They were to teach only that which
Church leaders had written and that which was given them
by the Spirit. (Verse 9.) The elders were told that even
though a person may appear outwardly humble, he is acceptable to God only if he keeps the commandments and brings
forth good fruits in his life. (Verses 15–19.) These missionaries did go to Missouri, arriving there in mid-July. (See
the discussion of sections 57 and 58 herein.)

Section 53: The Agent

The bishop had a weighty role in administering the tem-

Northeastern Ohio

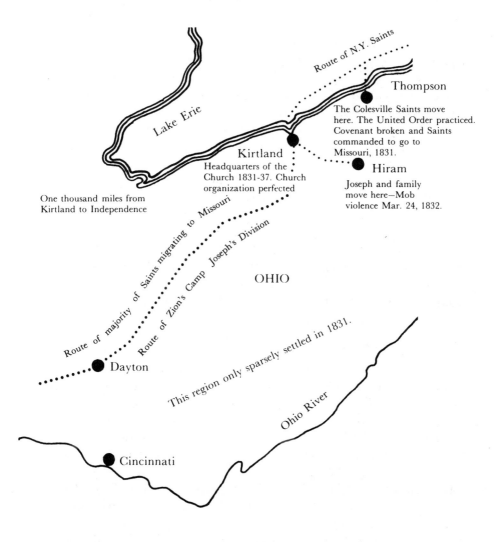

Route of N.Y. Saints

Thompson

The Colesville Saints move here. The United Order practiced. Covenant broken and Saints commanded to go to Missouri, 1831.

Lake Erie

Kirtland
Headquarters of the Church 1831-37. Church organization perfected

Hiram

Joseph and family move here—Mob violence Mar. 24, 1832.

One thousand miles from Kirtland to Independence

Route of majority of Saints migrating to Missouri

Route of Zion's Camp Joseph's Division

OHIO

This region only sparsely settled in 1831.

Dayton

Ohio River

Cincinnati

poral affairs of the Church under the law of consecration.
(See the discussion of the law of consecration under section
42 herein.) In this revelation, Sidney Gilbert was called to be
the first "agent" only four months after the revelation on
consecration had been given. The Lord later explained (D&C
84:113) that the agent was to take charge of secular or temporal business affairs under the direction of the bishop.

Section 54

When the branch from Colesville, New York, settled in the
vicinity of Thompson, Ohio, they entered a covenant with
Leman Copley and Ezra Thayre, who owned land in the
area, to organize themselves into an order according to the
law of consecration. (See discussion of consecration under section 42 herein.) When Copley and Thayre subsequently
backed out of the agreement and not all of the Colesville
Saints were faithful to their covenant, confusion resulted.
Their branch president, Newel Knight, sought counsel from
Joseph Smith, and section 54 was given. The Savior said he
would excuse those who were prevented from keeping their
covenant with him, but would hold accountable those who
were responsible for the breaking of the covenant. (Verses
4-6; compare D&C 124:49-50.) The Colesville Saints were
directed to move on to Missouri, where they played a key
role in laying the foundations of the work there. (See discussion of sections 57-58 herein.)

Section 55 and W. W. Phelps

When William W. Phelps came to Kirtland in mid-June of
1831 with the desire to do the Lord's will, this revelation was
received for him. He was first told to be baptized and was
promised ordination as an elder on condition of worthiness.
(Verses 1-3.) The Lord took advantage of Phelps's previous
experience as an editor by calling him to assist Oliver Cowdery in the work of printing (verse 4); Brother Phelps became the editor of the Saints' first newspaper, the *Evening and
Morning Star*, published in Independence, Missouri. His call to
assist in preparing books for school children reflected an
early Church interest in education. (Verse 4; see the dis-

W. W. Phelps (Photo courtesy Harold B. Lee Library)

cussion of the School of the Prophets under section 88 herein.) Elder Phelps also wrote the words to some of the best
known Latter-day Saint hymns, including "Redeemer of Israel," "Now Let Us Rejoice," "Praise to the Man," and "The
Spirit of God."

Section 56

The Lord had called Thomas B. Marsh to go with Ezra
Thayre (D&C 52:22) and Newel Knight to go with Selah
Griffin (52:32) as missionaries to Missouri. Meanwhile, be-
cause of the land disagreement in Thompson (see section 54),
Thayre apparently had lost the spirit of his calling, and
Knight had been told to go with his branch to Missouri.
Therefore the Lord reassigned Marsh and Griffin to serve as
missionary companions.

In verse 4 the Lord speaks of revoking his own commandments. Because he and his purposes are unchanging, and
man is constantly changing, he modifies his instructions so as
to accomplish his eternal goals in a variety of situations.

Proper Attitude about Wealth (Verses 16–18). These verses teach that it is not the presence or absence of wealth, but rather one's attitude towards it, that is either good or bad. (See "Seek Not for Riches" under section 6 herein.)

Sections 57–58: The Land of Zion

Old Testament prophets spoke of two latter-day gathering places from which the Lord's law and word should go forth: Jerusalem and the New Jerusalem, or Zion. (See Isaiah 2:2–3; Micah 4:1-2.) The Book of Mormon made it clear that while the ancient Jerusalem would be rebuilt and become the Holy City of the Lord in the Old World, the New Jerusalem would be built on the American continent. (Ether 13:4–6.) As early as 1830, the year in which the Church was organized, the building of the New Jerusalem was a subject of great interest, and the Latter-day Saints were eager to know just where the Holy City was to stand. In September of that year, Hiram Page had professed revelations making known, among other things, where the New Jerusalem or Zion would be located. (See the discussion of these circumstances under section 28 herein.) On that occasion, the Lord declared through his prophet that the location of Zion had not yet been revealed, but that it was "on the borders by the Lamanites" and that the exact location would be made known later. In the same revelation Oliver Cowdery was called to go as a missionary to the Lamanites. (See D&C 28:8–9.) Cowdery and his fellow missionaries traveled as far west as the "borders by the Lamanites" in western Missouri. (See the discussion of this mission under section 28 herein.) During the spring of 1831, the Lord directed his people to prepare to purchase land in the "western countries" where the New Jerusalem or Zion would be built. (See D&C 45:64–67.) On June 7, 1831, following a very spiritual conference, the Lord directed many of the elders to go to Missouri, the land the Lord had consecrated for the people of Israel, and it would be made known where their inheritances should be. (See D&C 52:1–5.)

In compliance with the above instructions, Joseph Smith

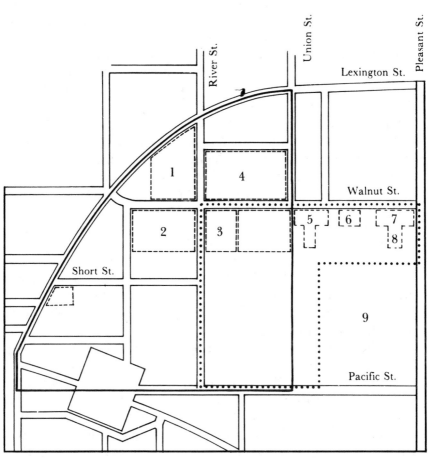

Church of Christ (Temple Lot) 1

Reorganized LDS Auditorium 2

LDS Visitors Center 3

Proposed RLDS temple site 4

New Independence, Mo., Stake Center 5

Mission Home Residence 6

LDS Chapel (Dedicated 1914) 7

Mission Office 8

RLDS "The Campus" Property 9

LDS Church ownership••••••••

63+ acres, included in the Saints' original 1831 purchase ⸻

Independence Temple Area

and many others left Kirtland in mid-June and arrived in
Jackson County, Missouri, just a month later. They had a
joyful reunion with the missionaries to the Lamanites and
with the many converts they had made in the area earlier in
the year. As the Prophet beheld the backward state of this
land and its inhabitants, he was moved to exclaim, "*When
will the wilderness blossom as the rose? When* will Zion be
built up in her glory, and *where* will thy temple stand?" Sections 57 and 58 were revealed, in part, to answer these questions. Section 57, verses 1–3, indicated the exact spot for the
temple lot. The accompanying map shows the boundaries of
the lands purchased for the Saints in 1831. Section 58, verse
3, however, suggested that the literal restoration of Zion
would come only "after much tribulation." Nevertheless these
early Saints had been brought to Missouri to test their obedience and in order that they might "be honored in laying
the foundation, and in bearing record of the land upon
which the Zion of God shall stand." (D&C 58:6–7.) The
"feast of fat things" and the "marriage of the Lamb" were
symbolic biblical prophecies of the Lord's second coming.
(Compare verse 8 with Isaiah 25:6, and verse 11 with Matthew 22:1–10 and Revelation 19:7.)

These two revelations contain many specific instructions
for those who were gathering to Zion at that time, particularly for the Colesville Branch which had been directed in
section 54 to continue its journey to Missouri. Members of
this group played a key role in the early Latter-day Saint
settlement of Jackson County. Twelve men, symbolizing the
tribes of Israel, carried the first log into place as building
commenced.

Today Latter-day Saints realize that they must be prepared both individually and as a church before Zion can be
built. Many of the instructions in these early revelations are
applicable to this present endeavor. (See section 105 for further consideration of requirements for establishing Zion.)

The Line Between "Jew and Gentile" (D&C 57:4). Early explor-
ers reported that the territory west of the ninety-fifth meridian (an imaginary north-south line a few miles west of Kan-

sas City, Missouri) was an arid, barren waste, totally unsuited for settlement. In light of these reports, the United States government adopted the concept of a "permanent Indian frontier" and from 1825 to 1840 followed the policy of removing Indians from east of this line and assigning them to reservations on the Great Plains. It was anticipated that non-Indian settlers would forever remain east of the ninety-fifth meridian, thus solving the problem of conflict with the Indians. (See Ray A. Billington, *Westward Expansion,* pp. 468–71.)

The "line running directly between a Jew and Gentile" mentioned in the Doctrine and Covenants was the adjacent portion of the "permanent Indian frontier," which was approximately the same as the western boundaries of the state of Missouri. The Lord used the term "Jew" to refer to the Lamanites or American Indians for the reasons explained earlier. (See "The Lamanites—a Remnant of the Jews" under section 19 herein.)

Obedience to Law (D&C 58:19–22). Those seeking to establish Zion must obey the law of God and should not break the law of the land. (See section 134 for a further consideration of the need to obey civil law.)

Initiative (D&C 58:26–33). Those engaged in building Zion cannot wait to be "commanded in all things," but must be "anxiously engaged in a good cause." The "slothful servant" who must always be prodded never can rise above the level of drudgery. On the other hand, those who go the "second mile" (Matthew 5:41) experience the joy which comes from freely giving of oneself. This is an illustration of the principle that blessings are conditioned upon our behavior. (See, for example, D&C 82:10 and 130:20–21.)

Furthermore, the Lord has worked through his "wise" and "anxiously engaged" servants to effect important developments in his work on earth. Some examples from Church history include Joseph Smith and the First Vision, Richard Ballantyne and the Sunday School, Aurelia Spencer Rogers and the Primary, Harold B. Lee and the Welfare Plan, to cite only a few illustrations. Within guidelines given in hand-

books and by those who preside over us, we should actively seek divine inspiration to help us to do "many things of
their own free will, and bring to pass much righteousness."
(Verse 27.)

The Nature and Fruits of Repentance (D&C 58:42-43). One of
the best brief definitions of repentance to be found in the
standard works is contained in section 58:43 (for a discussion
on the confession of sins, see p. 72). Verse 42 states (1) that
those who repent will receive forgiveness for their sins (see
discussion of forgiveness under section 19 herein), and (2)
that the Lord will remember the sins no more. Alma's experience shows that the individual may still remember his past
sins, but that after they have been forgiven they will trouble
him no more. (See Alma 36:19-21.) The Lord has warned,
however, that if one sins again, the former sins will return.
(See D&C 82:7.)

Section 59: The Lord's Day

Soon after the arrival of the Colesville Saints, Sister Polly
Knight (wife of Joseph Knight, Sr.) passed away, the first
Latter-day Saint to die in the land of Zion. Her funeral was
held on Sunday, August 7, 1831. It was in this setting that
section 59 was received. Verses 1-4 were a message of comfort and encouragement to the Saints. Beginning in verse 5,
the Lord reviewed with them some of the basic commandments which can be grouped under the two great commandments—love of God and love of neighbor. Verse 21 warns
that one should recognize the Lord's hand in all things, and
verse 23 summarizes the fruits of righteous living in a most
meaningful way.

Observing the Lord's Day (Verses 9-15)

Purposes of the Lord's Day (Verses 9-10). Keeping the Sabbath
day holy is the commandment which received the greatest attention. In contrast to the common tendency to think in
terms of what one cannot do on Sunday, section 59 stresses
the positive aspects of the day. Verse 10 suggests two principal purposes of the Sabbath:

1. To rest from one's daily labors.

2. To serve and worship the Lord.

In attempting to decide if a given activity is appropriate for the Lord's day, one might consider whether or not it interferes with or detracts from these major objectives.

Sunday Is the Lord's Day. The Lord set the pattern for Sabbath observance when he rested from his labors on the seventh day. (See Genesis 2:2–3.) He later made this one of the Ten Commandments. (See Exodus 20:8–11.) Following the exodus, the Hebrews had a fixed-date system of reckoning their Sabbath. This meant that certain dates during the years were set aside as Sabbaths; but because each year started one or two days later in the week than did the previous year, these Sabbaths fell on a different day each year. According to one student of the subject, the Jewish people did not adopt their custom of regularly observing Saturday as the Sabbath until after the destruction of Jerusalem in about A.D. 70. (For a full treatise on this subject, see Samuel Walter Gamble, *Sunday, the True Sabbath of God.*) The primitive church met on Sunday, the first day of the week, which they knew as the Lord's Day in honor of his having been resurrected on Sunday. (See John 20:19–29; Acts 20:7; 1 Corinthians 16:2; Revelation 1:10.) Section 59, which treats the Lord's Day, was given on Sunday. (See especially verse 12.)

Oblations (Verse 12). The word *oblation* refers to an offering made to the Lord in worship. In ancient Israel, sacrificial offerings were a means of directing the people's attention to the Lord's future great atoning sacrifice. Since that event, members of the Church have partaken of the sacrament as a means of remembering Christ's atonement. They have been commanded to make an offering of a "broken heart and a contrite spirit." (3 Nephi 9:19–20; D&C 59:8.) Thus, verse 12 associates the concept of oblations with partaking of the sacrament and manifesting repentance through confession of one's sins when appropriate.

"Fasting" (Verses 13–14). The word *fasting* normally refers to abstaining from food and drink. In these two verses, however,

the term is used in a unique sense, as is suggested by the instruction that food is to be "prepared with singleness of heart that thy fasting may be perfect." Verse 14 clarifies the fact that in this particular passage *fasting* is used synonymously with *rejoicing*. In the Sermon on the Mount, the Lord disapproved of the custom of linking outward or public mourning with fasting. (See Matthew 6:16–18.) When one realizes that fasting is a means of developing spirituality, rejoicing rather than mourning seems to be most appropriate.

Sections 60–61: The Return Trip from Zion

On Monday, August 8, 1831, as the brethren from Ohio were preparing to return home, section 60 was received in which return travel instructions were given. The elders were told to go by river to St. Louis (D&C 60:5), from which point some were to continue speedily to their homes, but most were to preach along the way as they went. Joseph Smith and ten other elders left Independence the next day. On Thursday afternoon, dangerous conditions were encountered on the river, and manifestations of Satan's power and presence were experienced. The following morning, section 61 was received to explain these things and also to elaborate on further travel directions.

Congregations of the Wicked (D&C 60:8 ff.). Instructions for the missionaries to preach among the congregations of the wicked do not mean that they were necessarily to seek out the worst elements of the population. The Lord used the word "wicked" to refer to all the inhabitants of the earth who had not yet accepted the fulness of the gospel, perhaps many never having even heard it. (See D&C 35:12; 84:49–53.) The word *gentiles* has sometimes been used in much the same sense as the Lord has used the term *wicked* here, in referring to those who had not become part of the covenant people.

Travel by Water (Section 61). The Lord explained that he had allowed the group to come by water that they might better be able to bear witness to the dangers on the water, particularly upon the western rivers in that vicinity. (See verses 4–5.) Because Satan's power was upon the waters (verse 19), those whose faith might fail them should avoid these waters lest they be "caught in snares." (Verse 18.) Those whose faith is strong will not only have power to command the waters but will also be led by the Spirit. (See verses 27–28.) In such cases, it would not matter whether they went by water or by land, as long as they fulfilled their missions. (See verse 22.)

Section 62

The Lord had told a group of the Missouri missionaries that he was not pleased with some of them because "they will not open their mouths, but they hide the talent [testimony?] which I have given unto them, because of the fear of man." (D&C 60:2; see also verse 13.) In section 62, the Master addressed another group which was still on its way to Missouri. He assured them that: "Ye are blessed, for the testimony which ye have borne is recorded in heaven for the angels to look upon; and they rejoice over you." (Verse 3.)

He also approved the elders' riding rather than walking. (Verses 7–8.) In contrast to some small religious sects, the Lord's Church has always taken advantage of modern technology when by so doing his work would be expedited.

Section 63: On Going to Zion

Joseph Smith arrived back in Kirtland near the end of August 1831. He found that the building of Zion was the leading topic of interest among the Saints in Ohio. Sections 63 and 64 were both received within about two weeks of the Prophet's return, and, like sections 57 and 58, they contained many instructions for those who were to go to Missouri as well as for those who were to remain in Ohio.

Signs and Faith (Verses 7–12). This revelation agrees with teachings in the Bible which condemn those who base their faith on signs, often for selfish motives. (See Matthew 12:39.) Signs are not the foundation of, but rather follow, faith. (See Mark 16:17–18.) Alma taught that one who is compelled to be humble and have faith is not so blessed as one who humbles himself because of the Lord's word. In this spirit, signs would compel one to believe, so there would not be any room for faith. (See Alma 32:13–21.)

In this passage, *signs* might be thought of as being synonymous with miracles or wonders. These should not be confused with the *signs* or *signals* of the Lord's coming which the faithful are commanded to seek to understand.

The accompanying diagram helps illustrate why faith cannot be based on signs. Elder James E. Talmage pointed out that *"belief* ... may consist in a merely intellectual assent, while *faith* implies such confidence and conviction as will impel to action." Thus, belief is essentially passive, and faith is an active force. Specifically, we may transform belief in Christ into faith by pondering the word of God (Romans 10:17) and through prayer. Even this "beginning faith" is a product of revelation—a gift from God—which gives us an assurance of his existence and concern for us. Alma compared this faith to a seed which must be continually nourished (Alma 32:37), through keeping the commandments, praying, and searching the scriptures. As we gain more knowledge of the character and attributes of God, our faith becomes perfect. Joseph Smith taught in the "Lectures on Faith" that this knowledge makes our faith a principle of power—the same power by which the worlds were created and are now governed. Thus we can move from belief to perfect faith only by seeking the kind of knowledge or testimony which comes through the Lord's Spirit. Seeking for signs represents a deviation from this path. Receiving "proofs" through human senses or reason may give us a false sense of security. Elder Talmage pointed out that even "knowledge may be as dead and unproductive in good works as is faithless belief." The personal witness of the Spirit is required to transform even perfect knowledge into an active source of blessings for our lives.

	Imperfect Knowledge	Perfect Knowledge
Passive	Belief	Knowledge
Active	Beginning Faith (Alma 32)	Perfect Faith (Joseph Smith)

Fate of Liars, Sorcerers, and the Like. (Verses 17–18). According to this passage, such persons "shall have their part in ... the second death." This fate is generally thought to be reserved only for the sons of perdition. Doctrine and Covenants 76:103, on the other hand, suggests that these people will receive a telestial kingdom and are "thrust down to hell" or, in other words, consigned to the spirit prison where they suffer the torments of Satan until the second resurrection. (See D&C 76:84–85.) Because they are temporarily cut off from the presence of God and are in a condition of spiritual death and are subject to the buffetings of Satan, those in the spirit prison may be said to "have their part in ... the second death." Only those liars, sorcerers, and the like who also commit the unpardonable sin, and thereby become sons of perdition, will suffer the second death forever.

Future Conditions of the Faithful (Verses 20–21, 49–51): Earth to Be Transfigured (See verse 20). The earth will pass through two changes which might be called transfigurations:

1. At the beginning of the Millennium, it will be raised from its present telestial to a terrestrial state, and only the righteous will have a place on earth at that time.

2. After the thousand years are ended, the earth will be celestialized and the faithful who are worthy of that glory will receive their permanent inheritance thereon. (See Chart 10, "Various Stages of the Earth's History," under section 77 herein.)

Verses 49–51 refer to conditions at the beginning of the Millennium. (For a consideration of the Millennium, see the discussion under section 101 herein.)

Mysteries of the Kingdom: (Verse 23). Normally the faithful think of staying away from the mysteries. (For a discussion of this matter, see "The Mysteries of God Shall Be Unfolded unto You," under section 6 herein.)

Section 64

Like section 63, this revelation instructed the Saints in Ohio who were eager to learn more about establishing the latter-day Zion. Here again the Lord taught principles which are still vital for us today.

The Law of Forgiveness (Verses 1–17). The Lord said: "I, the Lord, will forgive whom I will forgive, but of you it is required to forgive all men." (Verse 10.) In many other revelations the Lord has made it clear that he will forgive all who repent.

Members of the Church should forgive their fellowmen if they expect the Lord to forgive them; this is in agreement with the Lord's Prayer. (See Matthew 6:12.) When Peter asked if he would have to forgive his brother as many as seven times, the Lord told him that he should be prepared to forgive seventy times seven. (See Matthew 18:22.)

The Lord does not expect one to endure without limit if the offender is unrepentant. Section 64:12 suggests possible recourse to Church courts for satisfaction. Section 98 admonishes one to bear afflictions with patience, but also suggests that after a certain point, the individual is justified in taking action against his enemy. Nevertheless, if he continues in the spirit of forgiveness, the Lord will bless him greatly. (See D&C 98:23–31.)

Section 65: The Kingdom of God

Like section 109, this section is a prayer given through revelation. It is always appropriate to ask the Lord to help one know what would be for his best good so that he might know for what to pray; in such cases, his prayer would reflect that which had been given to him by revelation.

The prayer in section 65 asks the Lord to help bring Daniel's prophecy to fulfillment. (See Daniel 2:26–45, especially verse 44.) Although the phrases *kingdom of God* and *kingdom of heaven* are sometimes used interchangeably, it is apparent in section 65 that the *kingdom of God* is the earthly organization which is to prepare the way for the Lord and his heavenly kingdom. Although at present the kingdom of God or the Church is concerned with spiritual matters, it will also embrace political affairs by the time the Savior comes in glory. (See Sperry, *Compendium,* pp. 274–83.)

Section 66

During the summer of 1831, William E. M'Lellin (pronounced and sometimes spelled McLellan) was converted by Samuel Smith and accompanied the elders on their mission to Missouri. He then returned to Kirtland seeking to know the Lord's will. In this revelation he was not only called to further service, but he was also warned about a serious temptation which had been a problem in the past. At a special conference held only a week later, M'Lellin challenged the wording of the Lord's revelations. (See the discussion of section 67 below.)

Ultimately, however, Brother M'Lellin must have heeded the Lord's warning, because he was later selected as one of the original Twelve Apostles in this dispensation.

Section 67: The Special Hiram Conference of 1831

A conference was convened in Hiram, Ohio, on November 1 and 2 of 1831 to consider the publication of revelations thus far received. Section 67 was received in relation to events which transpired at the conference.

Sequence of Events at the Conference

1. The brethren decided to publish 10,000 copies of the Book of Commandments. The size of the edition was reduced to 3,000 at another conference the following year.

2. Several of the brethren present testified that the Spirit had borne witness to them that the revelations were true, and they expressed their desire to declare this testimony to the world.

3. The Lord, the book's true author, gave a revelation in which he testified that the compiled revelations were true. This revelation, designated "The Lord's Preface," now stands as section 1.

4. There followed a discussion on the language in the revelations about to be published. Criticisms of Joseph Smith's language aroused doubts in the minds of some of the brethren present. These concerns may have been related to the popular belief that God had dictated the scriptures word for

word; thus, questions about the language represented a lack of faith in the divine origin of the revelations.

5. In a revelation (section 67), the Lord acknowledged the feeling of the critics and challenged them to select the wisest man present and have him try to duplicate the least of the revelations given through the Prophet. If the man was successful, the others would know they were no longer obligated to bear witness to the truthfulness of the compiled revelations. Being able to duplicate one of the Lord's revelations would mean more than merely imitating the literary style of their revelations, but would also include being able to duplicate the spirit of the genuine revelations, and like them, bring forth new and divinely inspired concepts.

6. Joseph Smith recorded that after the foregoing was received, William E. M'Lellin—as the wisest man in his own estimation, having more learning than sense, endeavored to write a commandment like unto one of the least of the Lord's but failed; it was an awful responsibility to write in the name of the Lord. (*HC,* 1:226; see also pp. 222–27.)

7. The elders renewed their desire to bear witness to the truth of the revelations. Joseph Smith then received the testimony now appearing in the "Explanatory Introduction" to the Doctrine and Covenants, page iv.

8. Within a day of the end of the conference, sections 68 and 133 were given. The latter has been designated "the Appendix" and, therefore, stands near the end of the compilation.

Seeing the Face of God (Verses 10–12). The Doctrine and Covenants lists several conditions which must be met if God is to be seen. God has never been seen except by the power of the priesthood (D&C 84:19–22), and one must abide the law in order to endure God's glory (D&C 88:21–24). Section 67 makes it clear that if one in the flesh is to see God, he must be quickened by the Spirit because neither *carnal* mind nor *natural* faculties could behold God's glory. The word *carnal* literally means "pertaining to the flesh," but in the scriptures also conveys the idea of worldliness or sinfulness in contrast to spirituality. (See Romans 8:6.) The term *natural* has a similar meaning. In the King James Version, Paul wrote: "The natural man receiveth not the things of the Spirit of God" (See 1 Corinthians 2:7-14.) The Revised Standard Version uses the word *unspiritual* rather than *natural* in this passage. King Benjamin suggested a similar meaning: "For the *natural* man is an enemy to God, and has been from the fall of Adam, and will be, forever and ever, unless he yields to the enticings of the Holy Spirit, and putteth off the natural man and becometh a saint through the atonement of Christ." (Mosiah 3:19; italics added.) Moses also explained that when he saw the Lord he had to be transfigured or quickened by the Spirit, for his natural eyes would never have beheld. (Moses 1:11.)

Section 68

This revelation was received within a day or so following the conference which had decided to publish the compiled revelations. Verses 1-12 were received specifically for the guidance of four missionaries who were about to depart. Verse 13, however, suggests that the balance of the revelation consists of Addenda to the "covenants and commandments" (another title for the Book of Commandments which was about to be published). Items in these later verses are particularly related to the content of section 20, which, with section 22, had been accepted as the "articles and covenants" of the Church.

What Is Scripture? (Verses 2-4). These verses, directed to a group of missionaries, specify two general requirements which must be met if a pronouncement is to be accepted as "scripture": (1) It must be inspired, and (2) it must be within the jurisdiction or authority of the one making the pronouncement. Thus a bishop may receive "scripture" for his ward, or a stake president for his stake. Similarly, worthy fathers bearing the holy priesthood should receive "scripture" for their families. Of course, only the president of the Church may receive "scripture" for the whole Church or for the world. President J. Reuben Clark, Jr., declared:

Only the President of the Church, the Presiding High Priest, is sustained as Prophet, Seer, and Revelator for the Church, and he alone has the right to receive revelations for the Church, either new or amendatory, or to give authoritative interpretations of scriptures that shall be binding on the Church, or change in any way the existing doctrines of the Church. He is God's sole mouthpiece on earth. . . . He alone may declare the mind and will of God to his people. ("When Are Church Leaders' Words Entitled to Claim of Scripture?" *Church News*, July 31, 1954.)

Elder Ezra Taft Benson suggested three tests by which we can judge the authenticity of any statement: (1) "What do the standard works say about it?" Any new statement must be consistent with the eternal principles revealed in the scriptures. (2) What do the latter-day prophets, particularly the living president, have to say on the subject? (3) Our own personal witness through the Holy Ghost is the final test. D&C 50:22 declares that those who teach and those who listen by the Spirit "understand one another, and both are edified and rejoice together." (*CR*, October 1963, pp. 16–17.)

The "Signs of the Times" (Verse 11). Latter-day Saints are not only privileged, but are also commanded, to ponder and heed the signs of the Savior's approaching coming in glory. (See the discussion of section 45 herein.)

Selecting Bishops (Verses 14–24). At the time this revelation was received, only one bishop, Edward Partridge (see section 41), was serving. The promise of "other bishops" was fulfilled beginning in the following month with the call of Newel K. Whitney. (Section 72.) The "legal right" of literal descendants of Aaron to this office is related to the organization of the lesser priesthood during Old Testament times. (See the discussion of the office of bishop and the history of the priesthood under section 107 herein.) Note that these verses contain the first reference to the "First Presidency" in latter-day revelation. Provisions in verses 22–24 regarding the trial of bishops refer only to the Presiding Bishop.

Parents' Responsibility (Verses 25–28). The prime responsibility of teaching children the gospel rests with their parents. Church leaders have frequently cited these verses in support of the family home evening. Parents who fail to teach their children must assume responsibility for the children's transgressions. (Compare Jacob 1:18.) Here, for the first time, the Lord specifies the precise age of accountability. (See the discussion on the status of little children under section 29 herein.) Verse 25 contains the first Doctrine and Covenants reference to stakes of Zion; the first stake was organized in Kirtland just over two years later. (See the discussion of section 102 herein.)

Section 69

Church leaders had appointed Oliver Cowdery to take the manuscript copy of the revelations to Independence for publication; he was also to carry a large sum of money to the Saints in Missouri. As a security measure, John Whitmer was here called to go with Elder Cowdery to help protect him in his travel to the frontier. The Lord also gave Brother Whitmer further instructions concerning his earlier assignment to keep a Church history. (See the discussion of section 47 herein.)

Section 70

The Lord in this revelation directed that those who had worked on the project should derive their temporal support from the publication of the compiled revelations. He further suggested that those who administer spiritual things should be equal in receiving temporal support with those who administer temporal affairs. (See "Remuneration for Church Service," p. 77.)

Section 71

During the fall of 1831, Joseph Smith went to live with the John Johnson family in Hiram, Ohio. Here he resumed the work of "translating" or revising the Bible. (See the discussion on "The Inspired Revision," under sections 30–36 herein.) In mid-September, it was learned that Ezra Booth had renounced his membership in the Church. He previously had been for some time a Methodist preacher "of much more than ordinary culture." He had joined the Church dur-

ing the spring of 1831 when he witnessed Joseph Smith heal
Mrs. Johnson's lame arm, a long-standing infirmity. During
the summer, Booth accompanied the missionaries going to
Missouri. (See D&C 52:23.) Joseph Smith recorded that
when Booth discovered that "faith, humility, patience, and
tribulation go before blessings," and that he could not command God to smite men in order to force them to believe,
"then he was disappointed." He published a series of nine
bitter anti-Mormon letters in the *Ohio Star* at Ravenna
(about thirty-five miles southeast of Kirtland). He was not
the first apostate to defect, but was probably the first to publish anything against the Church. (See *HC*, 1:215–17, 238–39,
including footnotes.)

It was in this setting that the Lord in section 71 directed
Joseph and Sidney to set aside their work of revising for
a time and go on a brief mission which had at least three
purposes:

1. To answer Booth's false charges; hence, the unusual admonition to "confound your enemies." (Verse 7.) Missionaries
generally try to avoid the spirit of contention.

2. To expound the mysteries, or, in other words, to preach
the gospel. (See verse 1; also discussion of mysteries under
section 6 herein.)

3. To prepare the people to receive the compilation of revelations to be published in the *Book of Commandments.* (See
verse 4.)

The brethren continued on this mission until the revelation
in section 73 directed them early in January 1832 to resume
their work revising the Bible. They had done "much towards
allaying the excited feelings which were growing out of the
scandalous letters then being published in the *Ohio Star.*"
(*HC*, 1:241.)

Section 72: The Second Bishop

Edward Partridge had been called ten months earlier (February 1831) to be the first bishop in the Church. (See D&C
41:9.) In the meantime, Bishop Partridge (D&C 58:24) and
Sidney Gilbert, an agent (D&C 64:18), had been directed to

Newel K. Whitney (Photo courtesy Harold B. Lee Library)

move to Missouri. This left nobody in Ohio to administer temporal affairs there. Thus, in August the Lord had called Newel K. Whitney to be the agent (D&C 63:42-45), and now, in December 1831, to be the bishop in Ohio (See D&C 72:8). Bishop Whitney was to render an accounting to Bishop Partridge, thus setting the pattern of a plurality of bishops, some having local jurisdictions working under a presiding bishop. Whitney was to "recommend" those who were worthy and who were going to Zion (verse 19); this may have been the beginning of the custom of calling one's membership records his "recommends."

This was the last section received during 1831, the year in which there were more Doctrine and Covenants revelations received than in any other single year.

Section 73

Section 71 had called Joseph Smith and Sidney Rigdon to go out and preach in order to answer false charges against the Saints. Now they were to return to their work of "translating." (See the discussion of Joseph's "New translation" or inspired revision of the Bible under sections 30-36 herein.)

The remainder of the elders were to continue preaching until the time of the conference which convened two weeks later. (See the discussion of section 75 herein.)

Section 74

Following the Lord's instructions in section 73, Joseph Smith resumed his "translation" or inspired revision of the Bible. Questions about the meaning of specific biblical passages became the occasion for receiving several revelations now in the Doctrine and Covenants (sections 74, 76, 77, 86, 91, and 113, for example). Section 74 is related to Paul's teachings about marriage in general, and contains the Lord's explanation of 1 Corinthians 7:14 in particular.

Paul's Teachings on Marriage

Marriage and the family are central in the faith of the Latter-day Saints. Because some critics claim that Paul disapproved of marriage, it is important to study his teachings thoroughly in order to determine what his true position really was. In 1 Corinthians 7, Paul identified certain portions as being his own opinion rather than being revelations from God. (See especially verses 6, 10, 12, and 25.) The instructions in verses 8-9 and 24-28 are most often cited in support of celibacy; note that they fall in parts of the chapter which Paul labeled as his own opinion. Knowing to whom Paul addressed these instructions should help one better understand their meaning. Joseph Smith's inspired revision of verse 29 supplies the following information: "But I speak unto you who are called into the ministry; for this I say, brethren, the time that remaineth is but short, that ye shall be sent forth unto the ministry. Even they who have wives, shall be as though they had none; for ye are called and chosen to do the Lord's work." These instructions concerning relations with the opposite sex correspond with present-day counsel to full-time missionaries who are "called unto the ministry."

In other passages Paul advocated marriage. For example, he counseled young widows to "marry, bear children and guide the house." (1 Timothy 5:14). It is apparent that Paul believed in celestial or eternal marriage when he wrote: "Neither is the man without the woman, neither the woman without the man, in the Lord." (1 Corinthians 11:11.)

Was Paul himself married? As a strict Pharisee, he would not have neglected so important a responsibility under Jewish law. Furthermore, marriage was a requirement for membership in the Sanhedrin, to which Paul probably belonged. In defending his standing as an apostle, Paul asserted his right to have a wife. (See 1 Corinthians 9:5.) Clement, an early Christian leader, wrote the following about apostles who were married: "Peter and Philip, indeed, had children; Philip also gave his daughters in marriage to husbands, and Paul did not demur in a certain epistle to mention his own wife [Philippians 4:3], who he did not take about with him, in order to expedite his ministry the better." (Eusebius, *Ecclesiastical History*, 7:8–9.) The word "yokefellow" in Philippians 4:3 is translated from the Greek word *syzygos*, which commonly means "wife." Commentaries written prior to A.D. 250 consistently interpreted this passage as referring to Paul's wife, while those written later have not given this interpretation.

Paul may have remained a widower after his wife died in order that he could devote more time to his calling in the ministry. (See Sidney B. Sperry, *Paul's Life and Letters*, pp. 9, 130–32.)

Interfaith marriages. First Corinthians 7:14, the verse enlarged upon in section 74, was part of Paul's teachings about mixed or interfaith marriages. Paul pointed out in verses 12–14 of 1 Corinthians 7 how a church member could, through his influence and example, convert his nonmember spouse and thereby bring the sanctifying blessings of the gospel into their family and save not only themselves but also their children from being subject to false traditions. Note that Paul did not advocate marrying an unbeliever; to the contrary, he recognized the inadvisability of contracting such relationships. (See 2 Corinthians 6:14.)

In section 74, after quoting 1 Corinthians 7:14 (in verse 1), the Lord proceeded to point out a pitfall in mixed marriages:

an "unbelieving" or non-Christian father, for example, could influence his children to follow the old Mosaic law rather than the gospel of Christ, and thus deprive them of its sanctifying blessings.

Section 75

During the early years of the Church, it was customary for many elders to do missionary work during the winter when they were unable to do their farming. Section 73 had directed the elders to continue preaching until they should receive new missionary appointments at the conference which was to be held in Amherst, Ohio, on January 25, 1832. It was at this conference that Joseph Smith was first sustained as President of the High Priesthood, the first high priests having been ordained at the conference held the previous June. This was the setting for the instructions received in section 75.

The elders were told to "shake off the dust of your feet" as a testimony against those who rejected their message. Missionaries still perform this ceremony today but are counseled to do so only when prompted by the Holy Ghost. In such cases the elders would be "filled with joy and gladness" (verses 20-21), not because they would see people condemned at the judgment, but because of their assurance that they were the Lord's authorized representatives, and as such, they had the power to bless those who accepted the gospel message (see verse 19). The missionaries were not to leave without first caring for their families, and it was the Church's duty to assist. Those who were obligated to remain at home to take care of their families were told to do so and to labor in the Church locally, and were assured they would not lose their blessings. (See verses 24-28.)

Section 76: "The Vision"

This section is unique in that it was revealed in a series of marvelous visions. Section 76 may be outlined for convenience in study:

1-10   The Lord's introductory greeting.

After the vision closed, Joseph Smith observed: "Nothing could be more pleasing to the Saints ... than the light which burst upon the world through the foregoing vision. ... Every honest man is constrained to exclaim: 'It came from God.' " (*HC,* 1:252-53.)

Section 76 was received in the home of John Johnson in Hiram, Ohio. Philo Dibble, a close associate of the Prophet who was in the room during much of the time while Joseph and Sidney were seeing the vision, has left the following eye-witness account:

Joseph would, at intervals, say: "What do I see?" as one might say

Johnson home in Hiram, Ohio. Here section 76 and others were received. (Photo courtesy LDS Church archives)

while looking out the window and beholding what all in the room could not see. Then he would relate what he had seen or what he was looking at. Then Sidney replied, "I see the same."

Presently Sidney would say, "What do I see?" and would repeat what he had seen or was seeing, and Joseph would reply, "I see the same."

This manner of conversation was repeated for short intervals to the end of the vision. And during the whole time not a word was spoken by any other person . . . not a sound or motion made by anyone but Sidney, and it seemed to me that they never moved a joint or limb during the time I was there, which I think was over an hour, and to the end of the vision.

Joseph sat firmly and calmly all the time, in the midst of a magnificent glory, but Sidney sat limp and pale, apparently as limp as a rag. Observing such at the close of the vision, Joseph remarked smilingly "Sidney is not used to it as I am." (Instructor, vol. 27, p. 303; quoted in Carter E. Grant, *The Kingdom of God Restored*, chap. 27.)

Inspired Revision of John 5:29 (Verse 17). As the brethren were revising the Bible, they questioned the traditional doctrine of "one heaven and one hell" in general, and the meaning of John 5:29 in particular. The correct meaning of this verse was restored as follows (italics added):

John 5	Section 76
29. And shall come forth; they that have done good, *unto* the resurrection of *life*; and they that have done evil, *unto* the resurrection of *damnation*.	17. They who have done good *in* the resurrection of the *just*, and they who have done evil *in* the resurrection of the *unjust*.

Thus the inspired version of the verse shifts the emphasis from two ultimate conditions to the idea of two resurrections. The whole section elaborates on this theme and gives an enlarged view of the four final kingdoms.

Testimony of Jesus Christ (Verses 22–24). This testimony of the glory of the Father and the Son is a fitting introduction to the entire revelation, and it stands in marked contrast to the vision of the sons of perdition which follows immediately afterward. Joseph and Sidney considered their witness to be a climax of all the testimonies which had been given because they were eyewitnesses. Their knowledge may be contrasted with the weak stand taken by those who argue that "God is dead," because the latter have personally never seen him. Verse 24 echoes a truth earlier revealed to Moses—that innumerable worlds are peopled with the sons and daughters of God. (Compare Moses 1:33–34.) The Prophet Joseph Smith later composed a poetic paraphrase of section 76. Expanding on the thought in verse 24, he declared that Christ is the Savior as well as the creator of these worlds:

And I heard a great voice bearing record from heav'n,
He's the Savior and Only Begotten of God;
By him, of him, and through him, the worlds were all made,
Even all that career in the heavens so broad.

Whose inhabitants, too, from the first to the last,
Are sav'd by the very same Savior of ours;
And, of course, are begotten God's daughters and sons
By the very same truths and the very same powers.

(*Times and Seasons*, February 1, 1843, pp. 82–83.)

The Four Final Kingdoms

Chart 9, on page 117, provides a convenient way to organize the information revealed in section 76 and related scriptures.

The names and symbols of these kingdoms are intended to identify conditions rather than locations. For example, the *celestial* (meaning "heavenly") kingdoms will be located on this earth (D&C 88:17–20), while the *terrestrial* (meaning "earthly") kingdom will be located elsewhere. Even though some stars are actually brighter, our sun appears to us to be the brightest object in the heavens and hence is the symbol for the most glorious kingdom. (For additional insight, see Joseph Fielding Smith, *Doctrines of Salvation*, vol. 2, pp. 20–48; Sperry, *Compendium*, pp. 334–62; *Commentary*, pp. 441–71; Melvin J. Ballard, *Three Degrees of Glory*.)

Sons of Perdition (Verses 25–49)

Status of Satan (Verses 25–29). Various titles reflect Satan's status before and following his fall. He was "Lucifer" (meaning "light bearer," "morning star"), "*a* son of the morning" (not "*the* son of the morning"), "who was in authority in the presence of God." Nevertheless he rebelled against the Father and became "Satan" (from Hebrew words meaning "enemy," "plot against"—compare Moses 4:1–4), or the "devil" (from Greek *diabolos* meaning "slanderer"). He was called "Perdition" (meaning "complete loss or ruin"). The description of his fall constitutes a solemn warning against departing from the path which leads to the celestial kingdom.

One may qualify as a son of perdition only by denying and defying the Lord's spirit and power after having known them. (Verses 31, 35.) For a consideration of this "unpardonable sin," see the discussions under sections 19 and 132 herein.

Lake of Fire and the Second Death (Verses 36–37). Whenever a person sins, he brings a condition of spiritual death upon himself in that he thereby impairs his ability to communicate with the Lord. Through the atonement of Christ, spiritual death will be overcome for all people, at least temporarily while they are brought into God's presence to be judged according to their works. Those who have committed the unpardonable sin will be cast out of the Lord's presence to be cut off forever from his glory or influence; this is what the scriptures call the "second spiritual" death, suffered permanently only by the sons of perdition. (Helaman 14:15–18.) The Book of Mormon clarifies the fact that references to a lake of fire and brimstone are only symbolic representations of the second death. (See 2 Nephi 9:16; Alma 12:17. King Benjamin taught that the torment is a sense of anguish for guilt—Mosiah 2:38; 3:25–27.) The Hebrew prophets wanted to compare eternal damnation to the worst possible place known to the people at that time. Gehenna, a sulfurous dump outside Jerusalem where garbage was continually being consumed by fire, became a most fitting symbol. (*D&C Commentary*, pp. 453–54.)

Chart 9

Four Final States

Three Degrees or Kingdoms of Glory			
Name	Celestial	Terrestrial	Telestial	Perdition
Meaning of Name	Heavenly	Earthly	"End" (i.e., last) or "Distant" (i.e., from God)	Complete loss
Symbol	Sun	Moon	Stars	Darkness
Requirements: Reaction to the Gospel	Valiant: overcome all things	Honorable, but "not valiant" in their testimony	Wicked who "receive not" (reject) the Gospel	Deny gospel after having sure knowledge from Holy Ghost
How Many Attain Each	"Many," but relatively few are exalted		Innumerable	"Many," but relatively few
Condition in Each Kingdom	Dwell with and have fulness of Father, Son, and Holy Ghost	Visits from the Son	Ministration of Holy Ghost via Terrestrial	With Satan and his angels. No contact with Godhead

Will the Sons of Perdition Be Resurrected? Verse 39 may suggest at first glance that only the sons of perdition will not receive a resurrection. The emphasis here is that they are the only ones who will not be *redeemed* from their personal sins, all the rest receiving a resurrection of *glory*. Doctrine and Covenants 88:32 makes it clear that even the sons of perdition will be quickened or resurrected. Alma taught that even though the wicked would suffer torment compared to a lake of fire, they cannot die because there is no physical corruption following the resurrection. (See Alma 12:17–18.)

Punishment of the Sons of Perdition (Verses 44–48). Verse 44 states that the sons of perdition are one group who will actually suffer "eternal punishment" eternally. (See discussion of "Eternal Punishment," p. 43.) Verse 48 does not teach predestination when it speaks of sons being ordained into this condemnation. Everyone has his free agency, but it is "ordained" that all who choose to transgress God's laws must suffer the consequences. (See Alma 42:22.)

The Celestial Kingdom (Verses 50–70, 92–96)

"In the celestial glory there are three heavens or degrees." (See section 131:1–4.) Exaltation refers only to obtaining the highest of these three divisions. In addition to the requirements for entering the celestial kingdom itself, one must also be faithful to the covenants of celestial or eternal marriage. (See discussion of celestial marriage under section 132 herein.) Those who are exalted become gods, and therefore must be prepared to carry out the works of a god—creating and populating worlds. Hence, the need for an eternal marriage relationship. The material in section 76 appears to refer specifically to those who will be exalted rather than all who inherit the celestial kingdom in general. (See especially verses 56–59 and 92–95.)

To attain exaltation, one must overcome all things through the atonement of Jesus Christ. Mortal language is inadequate to fully communicate the transcendent glory to be enjoyed by those who are exalted. Compare the promises in section 76 with other descriptions of the celestial world: D&C 77:1, 130:9; Joseph Smith's 1836 "Vision of the Celestial Kingdom" in the Pearl of Great Price, verses 2–4.

Sealed by the Holy Spirit of Promise (Verse 53). The "Holy Spirit of Promise" is the Holy Ghost, who ratifies and records ordinances which are received worthily. To those who qualify, he extends the promise of eternal life in the celestial glory. (See D&C 88:3–4 and 131:5.)

Church of the Firstborn (Verse 54 ff.) The Lord himself is the firstborn Son of God in the spirit. He has declared that all who are begotten through him partake of his glory and are

members of the "church of the Firstborn." (See D&C
93:21–22 and "Becoming the Children of God" under section
11 herein.)

The Terrestrial Kingdom (Verses 71–80)

The name *terrestrial* signifies "earthly." The terrestrial
kingdom will not be on earth, but it will be "earthly" in
the sense that its condition will be less than "heavenly"
(celestial).

Those Who Receive the Gospel in the Spirit World (Verses 72-74).
These verses seem to suggest that all those who receive the
gospel in the spirit world will be heirs of the terrestrial kingdom. If this were true, there would be no point in performing
temple ordinances for the dead, since those ordinances are
designed to qualify people for the celestial kingdom. Nevertheless, the Lord explained: "All who have died without a
knowledge of this gospel, who would have received it if they
had been permitted to tarry, shall be heirs of the celestial
kingdom of God." (D&C 137:7-9.) Still, it is possible that
those who were not as thoroughly prepared in the premortal
existence and who will ultimately inherit the terrestrial
kingdom may have been sent to the earth at a time and place
where they would not be required to live gospel laws for which
they were not ready.

The Telestial Kingdom (Verses 81–88, 98–112)

Meaning of "Telestial." This term is found only in writing
based on latter-day revelation. Elder James E. Talmage suggested that its meaning might be linked to the Greek word
telos, meaning "end." (See Talmage, *Articles of Faith,* p. 521.)
The apostle Paul stressed that each man will be resurrected
"in his own order," first Christ, later those who are "Christ's
at his coming," and finally "then cometh the end [telos]"
(See 1 Corinthians 15:21–24). Those who inherit the telestial
kingdom will come forth in the second or last resurrection.
Telestial might also be related to the prefix *tele* in such words
as telescope, television, etc., suggesting the idea of distance—
perhaps in this case distance from the throne of God.

"Receive Not the Gospel" (Verses 82–83). Because everyone will be given an opportunity to accept the gospel, the statement that telestial candidates "receive not the gospel" actually means that they *reject* it. These should be distinguished from those who *do* receive the gospel and then *deny* it, thereby becoming sons of perdition. (See verse 83.)

Even some who professed to be followers of Christ (verse 100) but who "received not the gospel, neither the testimony of Jesus" (verse 101), shall inherit the telestial kingdom.

"Thrust Down to Hell" (Verses 84–85). When these verses are read together, the "hell" spoken of in verse 84 seems to refer to the spirit prison rather than to Satan's permanent kingdom. The Book of Mormon uses the term "hell" in this same sense. (See 2 Nephi 9:11–13.)

Conclusion

Based on Law. In section 88, verses 17–39, one can read that each of these kingdoms is governed by law and that each person will inherit the kingdom whose law he has been willing to live. Verse 32 makes the interesting statement that the sons of perdition will "enjoy that which they are willing to receive, because they were not willing to [pay the price] to enjoy that which they might have enjoyed."

Progress from Kingdom to Kingdom? Using the concept of eternal progression, some have argued that it is possible to advance from a lower to a higher kingdom. The weight of evidence seems to be against this idea:

1. Doctrine and Covenants 76:112 states that heirs of the telestial kingdom can never go where God and Christ are.

2. Those who do not enter celestial marriage (which must be done during the second estate or probationary state) can never be exalted, even though they can become ministering angels in the celestial kingdom.

3. One is resurrected with the body suited specifically for the glory in one of the four final states, so he could not endure a higher glory for which his body is not prepared.

4. Belief in the possibility of progressing from kingdom to

kingdom would destroy the emphasis on this life being "the time for men to prepare to meet God." (Alma 34:32–35.)

Section 77: The Revelation of John

As the work of "translating" or revising the Bible went forward, the brethren had several questions about the revelation of John which are answered in this section.

History of the Earth (Verses 1, 6, 7). Chart 10 depicts the five distinct stages through which the earth will have passed.

1. It was first created as a spirit earth (Moses 3:5) in heaven, so was in a celestial state.

2. When it was created physically, it came into a terrestrial condition which lasted during the time Adam and Eve were in the Garden of Eden. Even though the earth was *physical* during this stage, it was *spiritual* rather than *fallen.* President Joseph Fielding Smith has pointed out that Adam was in a similar state before his transgression. (See *Doctrines of Salvation,* vol. 1, p. 93.)

3. Brigham Young taught that with the fall of Adam the earth also actually fell through space from its former location near the throne of God to its present orbit. (See *JD* 17:143.) This telestial, fallen condition is to last six thousand years.

4. Christ's second coming at the beginning of the seventh thousand years is to usher in his Millennial reign. (See verse 12.) The earth will return to the condition which existed while Adam and Eve were in the Garden. The term *paradise* has been used in some theological writing to refer to Eden; hence, the statement in the tenth Article of Faith: "We believe ... that the earth will be renewed and receive its paradisiacal glory." This thousand-year period will complete the seven thousand years of the earth's "temporal existence." (Verses 6 and 7.)

5. After the end of the Millennium the earth will be completely consumed by fire, in contrast to the beginning of the Millennium when it is only to be superficially cleansed by fire. It will become a celestial physical earth but will be spiritual rather than mortal or fallen in its nature. In this sanctified state it has been described as a "sea of glass" (verse 1)

Chart 10

Various Stages of the Earth's History

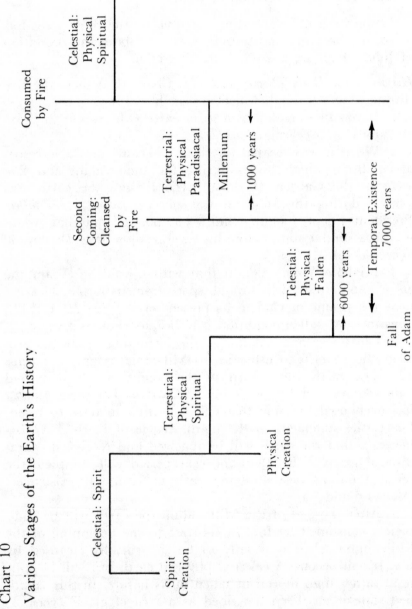

or as a "great Urim and Thummim" (D&C 130:6-9). (For a treatise on the history of the earth, see Joseph Fielding Smith, *Doctrines of Salvation,* vol. 1, chap. 5.)

Other Teachings Clarified: Verse 2 makes it clear that not only human beings but all living things have been created physically in the image of their spirits.

Joseph Smith taught that angels do not have wings. (See *Teachings,* p. 162.) Verse 4 gives the key that scriptural descriptions of heavenly beings' wings are only symbolic representations of their power.

Verses 9 and 14 refer to Elias, identifying John the Revelator as an Elias. (For a consideration of the uses of the word *Elias,* see section 27 herein.)

Verse 11 identifies the 144,000, thus correcting the error which exists in certain religious circles today.

Section 78: The United Order

In this revelation the Lord called a number of the leading brethren of the Church to unite by covenant and to form the "united order," an administrative body to coordinate and operate various business enterprises related to the law of consecration. (See discussion of the law of consecration under section 42 herein.) This should not be confused with the popular usage of the term "united order" in referring to the operation of the law of consecration as a whole, or to cooperative experiments in Utah during a later period of Church history. Section 82, beginning with verse 11, also gave further instructions concerning the united order.

Adam Holds the Keys (Verse 16). As the head of the human family, Michael or Adam was given the privilege of holding the keys of salvation under the direction of the "Holy One" (Jesus Christ). The *keys* are the power to direct the Lord's work on earth. They were passed down among the prophets, Elijah being the last to hold the keys of the higher priesthood and John the Baptist the last to bear the keys of the lesser priesthood before the coming of Christ. (See *Teachings,* pp. 172, 272.) The apostles received their priesthood directly from Christ (John 15:16) and received the keys from Moses and

Elijah on the Mount of Transfiguration (*Teachings,* p. 158). These same three apostles restored the keys as well as the Melchizedek Priesthood in this dispensation. Six years following the organization of the Church, Moses, Elias, and Elijah restored additional special keys. (See Section 110.) Just before Christ's second coming, a great priesthood conference will be held at Adam-ondi-Ahman, where all keys will be given back to Adam who will then turn them over to Jesus Christ in preparation for the Lord's personal reign on earth. (See Joseph Fielding Smith, *Way to Perfection,* chap. 40, p. 287.)

Son Ahman (Verse 20). Elder Orson Pratt has explained the meaning of this title. In the pure language, "Ahman" is the name of God, "Son Ahman" is the name of the Son, and "Sons Ahman" is the name of man. (See *JD,* 2:342.)

Sections 79–81

These revelations gave important calls to three brethren: Jared Carter, Stephen Burnett, and Frederick G. Williams. Frederick G. Williams's call as a counselor to Joseph Smith (section 81) was consummated just a year later with the organization of the First Presidency (section 90). Elder Williams became the Prophet's second counselor, holding the keys with him. (Compare D&C 81:2 with 90:6.)

Section 82

The spirit of rivalry had been manifest among some Church members, some of the leaders in Missouri feeling they were equal in authority to those in Ohio. These feelings centered on a personal antagonism between Bishop Edward Partridge in Missouri and Sidney Rigdon in Ohio. On a visit to Missouri during the spring of 1832, the Prophet was able to see these differences resolved, and the brethren in that place sustained him as President of the High Priesthood, as the Ohio brethren had done at the Amherst conference the previous January. It was in this setting of forgiveness and reconciliation that section 82 was received.

In the opening verses the Lord again stressed the importance of keeping his commandments (verses 1–10) and then turned to a further discussion of the united order (see section 78). In verses 12 and 13, the Lord spoke of Zion (Missouri) and of Kirtland as a "stake [or support] to Zion." This follows the usage of the word *stake* in Isaiah 54:2 as part of a comparison of Israel to a tent. The first regional "stake" unit was not organized at Kirtland for almost two years. (See section 102.)

Mammon of Unrighteousness (Verse 22). "Mammon" has been used in the scriptures as a symbol of worldliness. (See Matthew 6:24.) The direction to "make friends with the mammon of unrighteousness" certainly does not mean to adopt the sinful ways of the world; the Lord gave a similar injunction at the conclusion of a parable in which he had shown that even the wicked sometimes display wisdom which the righteous disciples would profit to copy. (See Luke 16:1–9.) This commandment may also suggest the importance of a friendly relationship before one can convert a sinner to righteousness.

Section 83

The prime responsibility of the family in caring for its members has been taught throughout various dispensations. See, for example, 1 Timothy 5:8 and Mosiah 4:14–15.

Section 84: Revelation on Priesthood

Priesthood and the Temple (Verses 1–42)

In his opening remarks, the Lord refers to the restoration of the gospel, to the building of the city of the New Jerusalem, and to the temple in which the sons of Moses and of Aaron would make an acceptable offering and sacrifice. When the Lord mentioned the sons of Moses in verse 6, he then inserted a lengthy explanation of the history and powers of the priesthoods (verses 6–30) before returning in verse 31 to the subject of the offering to be made in the temple. (The history, powers, and organization of the priesthood will be treated under section 107.)

The Office of Bishop as an Appendage to the High Priesthood

(Verses 29–30). Even though all offices are appendages to the Melchizedek Priesthood (D&C 107:5), it may seem confusing to see the office of bishop grouped with elders as appendages to the higher priesthood rather than with deacons and teachers as appendages to the lesser priesthood. One might think of the entire Aaronic Priesthood with the bishop at its head (D&C 107:87–88) as being, like the office of elder, an appendage to the Melchizedek Priesthood; while the offices of deacon and teacher, in turn, are appendages *within* the lesser priesthood.

Offering and Sacrifice (Verse 31). The "offering" may be the same as that mentioned in Doctrine and Covenants 128:24— an acceptable record of our dead. The "sacrifice" might refer to the offering of blood sacrifices on a very limited scale as part of the "restoration of all things." (See discussion under section 13, p. 32 herein; Sidney B. Sperry's excellent treatise on section 84 also gives valuable insight into these matters— see *D&C Compendium,* pp. 386–407.)

Oath and Covenant of the Priesthood (Verses 33–42). All who receive the priesthood should be familiar with the teachings in these verses. Those who are faithful and who magnify their calling in the priesthood are promised both physical and spiritual blessings; the "renewing" of the body mentioned in verse 33 may refer to an unusual endowment of good health and strength during mortality or to the resurrection when the body will be quickened by the Spirit according to the individual's degree of worthiness. (See D&C 88:25–32.) Faithful bearers of the Melchizedek Priesthood and Aaronic Priesthood will become the sons of Moses and Aaron, respectively, or, in other words, the sons of Levi (of whose tribe Moses and Aaron were members). All will be of the seed of Abraham and, therefore, heirs to the great blessings promised to his posterity. They are also described as the "elect of God" and are in line to receive his choicest blessings in time and in eternity. On the other hand, he warns that those who do not honor their priesthood will bring serious condemnation unto themselves.

Instruction to the Missionaries (Verses 43–120)

The Lord first counseled the elders to hearken to his words which represent the light of truth or *Spirit of Christ*. (See discussion of the **Spirit or Light of Christ, p. 131.**) Because of the wicked condition of the world, the Lord commanded the missionaries to go out and proclaim the message of the gospel. The Lord called these missionaries "friends" (verse 77) and in verse 88 further describes in a very beautiful way his close companionship with them.

Without Purse or Scrip (Verses 78–86). In contrast to the pattern of most denominations in which missionaries are salaried employees of their respective churches, the Lord wanted the elders to enter his service with a different spirit which is indicated in the directive to go forth "without purse or scrip." The word *scrip* means "satchel," "carrying bag," or a type of paper money; therefore, it may be a symbol of material (rather than spiritual) preparation. *Purse* may similarly be a representation of being overly concerned with worldly wealth.

Zion from Above and from Beneath (Verse 100). The missionaries were to look forward to the time when the Lord would bring "down Zion from above" (perhaps the city of Enoch whose return was prophesied in Moses 7:62–64) and also would bring "up Zion from beneath" (perhaps the city of Zion or New Jerusalem which is to built on the American continent).

Lesser Priesthood to Assist (Verse 107). The assignment suggested in this verse has been carried out by the Aaronic Priesthood Youth Missionary Committees organized throughout the Church during the 1960s.

Verses 108–110 and Priesthood Correlation. During the general conference in the fall of 1961, the Brethren announced a program through which the family would be acknowledged as the foundation for teaching and living the gospel. The priesthood was to assume a more significant role in selecting and implementing Church programs. All unnecessary duplication was to be eliminated, and each organization would then be helped to carry out more completely its unique role. In several of their talks on this subject, the General Authorities have used verses 108–110 of section 84 as a basic text.

Section 85: The One Mighty and Strong

Over the years, many apostates have arisen, each claiming to be the "one mighty and strong" whom the Lord was to send to set his house in order. (See verse 7.) The background for this revelation was a problem developing among the brethren in Missouri. Some who had gone were refusing to consecrate their property according to the Lord's command- ment. (See D&C 58:35–36; 72:15; etc.) The Lord warned that the names of the guilty would not be found among the genealogies or records of the Church or, in other words, that these people would lose their blessings as members of the Church. They would suffer the same fate as the transgressors mentioned in Ezra 2:61–62 who forfeited the birthright through which their children would have received the priest- hood. Apparently Bishop Edward Partridge had been lax in dealing with these offenders; it was to him that the Lord said he would send one mighty and strong to set in order the affairs in Zion. (See verses 7–8.) In 1905, the First Presidency issued a lengthy statement in which they explained that in light of section 85, if "one mighty and strong" were sent, he would assume the functions of the bishop in Missouri, thus disqualifying the many apostate claims. Bishop Partridge re- pented, however; so this warning never had to be carried out. (The First Presidency's statement is quoted in James R. Clark, comp., *Messages of the First Presidency*, [Salt Lake City; Bookcraft, 1970], 4:108–120.)

Section 86 and the Wheat and the Tares

The Savior used the parable of the wheat and the tares (Matthew 13:24–30) to describe the progress of his kingdom. It is instructive to compare his interpretation given in the Bible (Matthew 13:36–43) with that which he gave through latter-day revelation (section 86). The Doctrine and Cov- enants definitely places the parable in the context of the last days. (Verse 4.) This agrees with the inspired revision of the Bible. (See, for example, the Inspired Version, Matthew

13:41.) Note how this parable was also applied to the latter-day gathering of the Saints. (See D&C 101:64–75.) When the Savior was on earth, he himself was the sower of the good seed (Matthew 13:37), while in the latter days this role is taken by his apostles (D&C 86:2). Driving the Church into the Wilderness (D&C 86:3) had reference to the apostasy, while the Restoration has been described as calling forth the Church out of the wilderness (D&C 33:5). In section 86, the Lord declared that he was holding his angels back from cleansing out the wicked because his kingdom was still young. (Verses 5–7.) Nearly a half-century later, however, Elder Wilford Woodruff wrote that the time had come for the gathering out of the tares and that the Lord had released his angels to "reap down the earth." (*Young Women's Journal*, vol. 5, pp. 512–13; quoted in Doxey, *Latter-day Prophets and the Doctrine and Covenants*, vol. 3, pp. 127–37.)

Section 87: "Prophecy on War"

Joseph Smith's prophecy of wars beginning with the rebellion of South Carolina was given on Christmas Day, 1832, over twenty-eight years before the American Civil War began at Fort Sumter on Charleston Bay in South Carolina. Students of history realize that there was an earlier rebellion just one month before section 87 was received. For some time the Southern States, which depended heavily on imports from abroad, had resented the high tariff rates passed primarily to protect Northern manufacturing interests. In November 1832, the South Carolina legislature adopted an exposition which advanced the doctrine of the states' rights to nullify any act of the federal government which was not in their interest. In his journal entry prefacing the record of section 87, Joseph Smith referred to South Carolina's actions as a "rebellion." Some critics, therefore, argue that anyone in 1832 could have guessed that difficulties would begin in South Carolina and that the so-called South Carolina prophecy is not evidence at all of divine appointment. Joseph Smith, however, made it clear in a later statement that the South Carolina rebellion mentioned in section 87 was not the nullification controversy of 1832 but was still future. (See D&C 130:12–13.)

Other aspects of this prophecy are quite impressive. Joseph Smith referred to the South being divided against the North; at the time this prophecy was given, there were three contending sections—the Northeast, Southeast, and Northwest (Great Lakes area)—and it was uncertain along which lines alliances would be drawn. The Prophet also listed slavery and not the tariff as the dividing issue. The Southern Confederacy *did* call on Great Britain for assistance as prophesied in section 87.

Furthermore, one might wish to expand one's horizon from the American Civil War, in particular, to the wars which were to be poured out on the world in general. The history of warfare shows a marked acceleration from the time of the Civil War period. The concept of "total war" involving entire populations has replaced the former restricted involvement of only mercenary (or professionally hired) armies. The system of defensive alliances prophesied in verse 3 has become an essential fact in the present-day global scene.

"Lord of Sabaoth" (Verse 7). This Hebrew word is usually translated "hosts" (meaning "armies"), so this title denotes the Lord's being the ruler over all.

Stand in Holy Places (Verse 8). This injunction does not require the Latter-day Saints to spend all their time in such places as the temples and chapels; rather, Church members should, through their way of life, help make wherever they are a holy place.

Section 88: "The Olive Leaf"

This most significant revelation was given to a group of brethren who had assembled on December 27, 1832, to learn the Lord's will. About two weeks later, the Prophet wrote to the brethren in Zion (Missouri) and sent them a copy of this revelation, which he likened to the olive leaf plucked from the tree of paradise. The Prophet hoped that the lofty concepts contained in the revelation would help pacify the antagonisms which had been manifested among some of the brethren in Zion.

Promise of the Lord's Spirit (Verses 3-13)

There are several channels through which God can communicate his knowledge, power, and glory to man:

1. The *Light or Spirit of Christ* is the power or influence of the Godhead which radiates throughout the universe. (See verses 6-13.) Both the Holy Ghost and Light of Christ may be known as "the Spirit of God," "light of truth," etc. So the context must determine which meaning is intended.

2. The *Holy Ghost* is a male personage of spirit, the third member of the Godhead. His mission is to be in charge of the means of communication between the Godhead and mankind; his being only a spirit gives him advantage in carrying out this assignment. (See D&C 130:22.)

3. The *priesthood* is the power by which God created and now governs the universe; as such, it is closely related to the Light of Christ. As it is exercised among men, the priesthood may be defined as God's *authority* delegated to men by which they represent him, especially when performing special acts within his kingdom. Those who represent the Lord should seek to know what he would have them do; this knowledge comes through the Holy Ghost.

4. *Faith,* according to the Prophet Joseph Smith, is a principle of power—again, the power by which the worlds were made. (See his "Lectures on Faith.")

Thus, one can readily see the high degree of interrelationships which exist among these several media by which God's power is communicated. Rather than seeking to isolate one of these as the channel through which a given manifestation comes, one might rather wish to cultivate all of them in his life so that the Lord could more fully bless him. As an illustration, a person who is healed following an administration by the elders might have received the blessing either through his or the elders' faith, through their priesthood, or perhaps through the powers to heal or to be healed which are gifts of the Holy Ghost.

The Light of Christ. The Spirit or Light of Christ is manifest in a variety of ways. Section 88 (verses 6-13) describes it as being God's power which is in physical light and which also enlightens men's minds. Mormon describes it as the gift by which one can discern good from evil. (See Moroni 7:15–19.) Unlike the Holy Ghost, "whom the world cannot receive" (John 14:17) and whose influence is felt only on a limited basis, except by those who have received the laying on of hands, the Light of Christ "enlighteneth every man through the world" (D&C 84:45–46).

The influence which comes through the Light of Christ is less specific or intense than is the Holy Ghost's influence (See Chart 11.) The Light of Christ is one of the channels through which the Holy Ghost may communicate even secular knowledge to the world. Often people are led through the Light of Christ to the point where they are ready to receive a surer witness directly through the Holy Ghost.

It is probable that these manifestations of the Spirit are to be identified with the concept of "intelligence" and God's glory as discussed in section 93.

Gift of the Holy Ghost. The *gift* of the Holy Ghost is the *right,* if one is worthy, to have the constant companionship of the third member of the Godhead. The Holy Ghost does manifest himself on a limited basis as necessary to unbaptized persons, but only with the laying on of hands following baptism can one have the right to this influence on an unlimited basis. The words "receive the Holy Ghost" should be interpreted as a command, making it the individual's responsibility rather than merely his privilege to receive the Spirit. (Compare D&C 46:8.) Because the Holy Ghost is a spirit having definite form and size, he cannot be everywhere at once in person, but his influence can be everywhere present. Still, because he is a spirit, he can "dwell" in and quicken individuals as circumstances require (D&C 130:22); perhaps this type of ministration would be limited to very special occasions such as Joseph Smith's first vision. Thus, generally, when people speak of receiving the Holy Ghost, they would have reference to receiving his influence and power.

Holy Spirit of Promise. This is the Holy Ghost in his role as the

Chart 11

The Holy Ghost and the Light of Christ

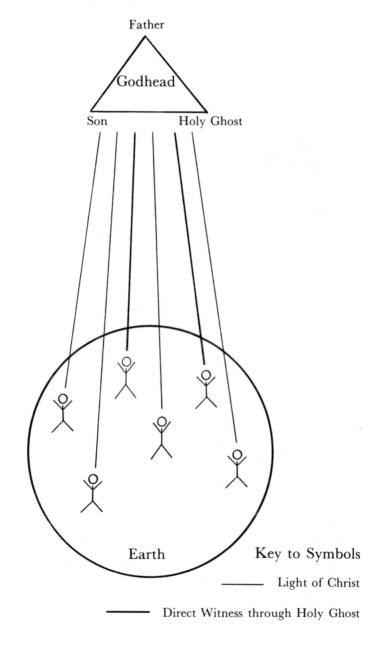

one who "seals" or ratifies ordinances in behalf of the worthy. Furthermore, when an individual has sufficiently proven
himself, he may receive "the promise of eternal life." (Verses
3-4; also D&C 131:5-6.)

The Second Comforter. When Jesus was about to depart from
his apostles, he promised to send them "another Comforter
. . . which is the Holy Ghost." (See John 14:16, 26.) In ana-
lyzing the fourteenth chapter of John, the Prophet Joseph
Smith pointed out that Christ promised still another Comforter—that Christ himself would also visit the apostles. (See
John 14:18.) This "Second Comforter" is Jesus Christ, who
may appear from time to time in person to those who have
received this gift. He, in turn, may manifest the Father unto
those who have attained such an exalted state of progression.
(See *Teachings,* pp. 150-51.)

President Joseph Fielding Smith has clearly discussed the
subject of the Holy Ghost, Second Comforter, Light of
Christ, etc., and their relationships in *Doctrines of Salvation,*
vol. 1, chap. 3.

Laws, Resurrections, and Kingdom (Verses 14-61)

Redemption of the Soul (Verses 14-15). As the individual enters
mortality, the spirit and body, the two component parts of
the soul of man (verse 15), are brought together. At death
they are separated, which may be thought of as a temporary
destruction of the soul as a unit. In this same sense, the resurrection is the "redemption of the soul," because through it
the spirit and body are inseparably joined together. Only
then can one experience a fulness of joy (D&C 93:33), because both spirit and body are essential to an individual's total development. Note that section 88 uses the term *soul* in a
very special sense; in other scriptural passages *soul* is used in
a more general sense as a synonym for *spirit.* (See Alma
11:40-45; 40:23.)

Kingdoms and Law (Verses 17-40). The Lord stated that each
kingdom is governed by law and that those who receive each
must abide its respective law. God the Father, knowing
through his own experience what course one must take in or-

der to achieve his goals, has given laws to mark the way along this path; therefore, God's laws should not be thought of as restrictive, but as showing the way to maximum achievement. Thus, "that which is governed by law is also preserved by law and perfected and and sanctified by the same." (Verse 34.) The Lord spoke of keeping the law as abiding "in the liberty wherewith ye are made free" and of breaking the law as becoming *entangled* in sin. (See verse 86.)

Evidence for God's Existence (Verses 41–50). These verses suggest that the principle of order in nature (such as the regular motions of the planets) is an *evidence* of God's existence, and therefore that those who have seen these things have, in a sense, seen him. (See especially verse 47; compare Alma 30:44.) *Proof* of his existence comes to each individual personally through the witness of the Holy Ghost and as prayers are answered. On the other hand, note that many who associated with Jesus Christ in the flesh did not acknowledge his divinity (verse 48); apparently they lacked the convincing witness of the Spirit. (For a discussion of how sure knowledge does and does not come, see sections 5 and 8–9 herein.)

Instructions to the Elders (Verses 62–86)

The Lord gave his "friends" significant instructions and beautiful promises related to personal preparation. (See particularly verses 63–69.) He then directed the elders to convene a "solemn assembly" in order that they might be prepared and sanctified. (Verses 70, 74.) This commandment is the underlying theme for the remainder of section 88.

Seek Knowledge (Verses 76–80, 118). The elders were directed to gather together in order to "teach one another." These verses, sometimes called "the charter of Church education," continue to guide educational programs. The elders were to seek learning by study as well as by faith. We should acknowledge that God knows all things about any branch of learning and that he can reveal these truths to us through the Holy Ghost. (See Moroni 10:5.) Nevertheless, we must prepare ourselves through effective study to receive and be able to comprehend that which he may reveal. The Spirit, in turn, provides an absolute standard by which we may judge the truth of ideas we study. Not only were the elders to learn "doctrine of the kingdom," but they were to become familiar with a variety of other subjects as well. (Compare verse 79 with D&C 90:15 and 93:53.) This knowledge would help the elders as well as us to be better prepared when called to serve. Hence, over the years the Church has valued education highly. (See the discussion on the "School of the Prophets" below.)

Responsibility to Warn Neighbors (Verses 81–82). Church leaders have quoted verse 81 often to emphasize Latter-day Saints' responsibility to share the gospel. The following verse implies that if we fail to do so, our neighbors might be able to excuse themselves for breaking commandments they did not know. Even as parents must assume responsibility when they fail to teach their children, perhaps also the Saints must bear some responsibility for the lives of their neighbors whom they fail to warn. The Book of Mormon records that Jacob and Joseph reached this same conclusion. (See Jacob 1:18–19.)

The Last Days (Verses 87–116)

To emphasize the importance of the ministry for which the elders were to prepare, the Lord inserted this lengthy discourse on latter-day events which soon were to occur. While section 45 gives an overview of the last days in general, these verses emphasize those events which are more particularly linked with Christ's second coming. The Lord warned that after the elders' testimony, would follow "the testimony of earthquakes," and so on.

Sign of the Son of Man (Verse 93). All mankind together shall see this great sign. (See Joseph Smith's inspired translation of Matthew in the Pearl of Great Price—Joseph Smith 1:24–26, 36.) Although the world will explain it away as being nothing more than an astronomical phenomenon (*Teachings*, p. 287), the prophets will declare that the sign is a warning to the Saints to prepare for the Lord's coming. (Orson Pratt, *JD*, 8:50.)

Order or Sequence in Resurrection (Verses 96–102). Even though every resurrected body will be physically perfect, not all will be prepared to enjoy the same degree of glory. (See the right-hand column of Chart 4, p. 29.) In his great chapter on the resurrection, Paul spoke of there being celestial, terrestrial, and other bodies. (See 1 Corinthians 15:40–42.) Earlier in the same chapter the apostle spoke of there being an order or sequence of resurrection. (See also 1 Corinthians 15:20–24 and John 5:28–29; Acts 24:15.) Section 88, verses 96-102, elaborate on Paul's statement.

Chart 12 illustrates the course which the history of resurrections will take. There will be two major phases:

1. The "first resurrection" or "resurrection of the just" began with the resurrection of Christ and will close with the end of the Millennium; those going to the celestial and terrestrial kingdoms will be resurrected during this phase.

2. The "second resurrection" or "resurrection of the unjust" will follow the Millennium and will include those who are going to the telestial kingdom and those who have become sons of perdition.

Only those going to the celestial kingdom are to be resurrected before Christ's second coming; this period is generally called the "morning of the first resurrection." There were a large number of persons resurrected at the time of Christ's resurrection. (See Matthew 27:52–53.) Since that time there have been relatively few come forth; but just before the Second Coming a large number of candidates for the celestial kingdom will be resurrected and "caught up" to descend with Christ in his coming in glory. (See D&C 76:63; 88:97–98.) For those who are living during the present dispensation, this great peak of celestial resurrections will be considered the "morning of our first resurrection."

Terrestrial resurrection will begin upon Christ's arrival when he comes to reign over the earth. Those going to this glory will be "Christ's at his coming." (Compare verse 99 with D&C 76:73.) These resurrections will then continue throughout the Millennium, this period being known as the "evening of the first resurrection." There will also be some

Chart 12

Sequence of Resurrections*

First Resurrection (Resurrection of the Just)		Second Resurrection (Resurrection of the Unjust)	
Morning	Evening		
Celestial	Terrestrial, Some Celestial	Telestial	Sons of Perdition
Resurrection of Christ	Second Coming	End of the Millennium	Final Judgment

*1 Corinthians 15:20-24, 40-42; D&C 88:22-32, 96-102.

celestial resurrections during this time—those who have lived as mortals during the Millennium on earth and who are worthy of the celestial kingdom, as well as those whose preparations in the spirit world were not yet complete when many of the celestial resurrections occurred at the beginning of the Millennium.

The rest of the dead will also be judged at the beginning of the Millennium but will be found unworthy so will spend the thousand years in the spirit prison and not be resurrected until the end of the Millennium. (Compare verses 100–102 with D&C 76:84–85.) There is no mention of a "morning" and an "evening" in the second resurrection, but it is probable that the same principle of orderliness will apply in this resurrection even as it did in the first. (For a discussion of the doctrine of resurrection, see Joseph Fielding Smith, *Doctrines of Salvation,* vol. 2, chap. 14–15.)

Further Instructions to the Elders (Verses 117–41)

In verse 117 the Lord returned to the subject of the solemn assembly to be held by the elders. The command to "establish a house" (verse 119) was fulfilled with the erection of the Kirtland Temple. Notice how verses 117–20 were repeated in the dedicatory prayer for that structure. (D&C 109:6–9.) In verses 118–26 he gave further instructions about personal preparation which are as meaningful and relevant today as ever. Finally, verses 127–41 outlined specific procedures to be followed in the "School of the Prophets."

The School of the Prophets (Verses 127–41). The concluding portion of section 88 sets forth the order and procedures to be observed in the School of the Prophets. Some of these instructions anticipated temple worship, which had not yet been restored.

Important Events in the School of the Prophets. The school was organized on January 22, 1833, less than four weeks after section 88 had directed its establishment. In accordance with instructions in this revelation, all who participated in the school were admitted by receiving the ordinance of the washing of feet, symbolizing their being clean from the sins of the world. (D&C 88:74, 138–39; *HC,* 1:323.)

According to Brigham Young, the School of the Prophets met in a small room, about 10 by 14 feet, situated above Joseph Smith's kitchen at the back of Newel K. Whitney's store. (*JD,* 12:157; quoted in Roy W. Doxey, *Latter-day Prophets and the Doctrine and Covenants,* 3:225–26.)

Sessions would begin about sunrise and continue until about 4:00 p.m. Those attending were instructed to bathe, put on clean linen, and come to school fasting. (Orlen C. Peterson, "A History of the Schools and Educational Programs of the Church . . . in Ohio and Missouri 1831–1939," [master's thesis, Brigham Young University, 1972], p. 23.)

Many important events occurred in meetings of the School of the Prophets. This is where section 89, the "Word of Wisdom," was first announced.

Significant spiritual manifestations blessed meetings of the School of the Prophets. The following occurred when the First Presidency was organized during one of the school's sessions:

March 18.—Great joy and satisfaction continually beamed in the countenances of the School of the Prophets, and the Saints, on account of the things revealed, and our progress in the knowledge of God. The High Priests assembled in the school room of the Prophets, and were organized according to revelation;

Elder Rigdon expressed a desire that himself and Brother Frederick G. Williams should be ordained to the offices to which they had been called, viz., those of Presidents of the High Priesthood, and to be equal in holding the keys of the kingdom with Brother Joseph Smith, Jun., according to the revelation given on the 8th of March 1833. [D&C 90:6.] Accordingly I laid my hands on Brothers Sidney and Frederick, and ordained them to take part with me in holding the keys of this last kingdom, and to assist in the Presidency of the High Priesthood, as my Counselors; after which I exhorted the brethren to faithfulness and diligence in keeping the commandments of God, and gave much instruction for the benefit of the Saints, with a promise that the pure in heart should see a heavenly vision; and after remaining a short time in secret prayer, the promise was verified; for many present had the eyes of their understanding opened by the spirit of God, so as to behold many things. I then blessed the bread and wine, and distributed a portion to each. Many of the brethren saw a heavenly vision of the Savior, and concourses of angels, and many other things, of which each one has a record of what he saw. (HC, 1:334–35.)

A "school of Elders" convened in Zion or Missouri during the late summer and autumn of 1833. Parley P. Pratt instructed these weekly sessions in a grove of trees. (See D&C 97:3–5: Parley P. Pratt, *Autobiography,* p. 93.)

A "school for the Elders" was conducted in Kirtland during the winters of 1834–35 and 1835–36. On December 1, 1834, Joseph Smith recorded the following concerning the first of these schools:

Our school for the Elders was now well attended, and with the lectures on theology, which were regularly delivered, absorbed for the time being everything else of a temporal nature. The classes, being mostly Elders gave the most studious attention to the all-important object of qualifying themselves as messengers of Jesus Christ, to be ready to do His will in carrying glad tidings to all that would open their eyes, ears and hearts. (HC, 2:175–76.)

The "lectures on theology" mentioned here are also known as the "Lectures on Faith" and were published with the Doctrine and Covenants prior to 1921. (See the last paragraph under "Explanatory Introduction" in the Doctrine and Covenants, p. v.)

When the Prophet opened the school's second season on November 3, 1835, he urged the elders to prepare for "the glorious endowment that God has in store for the faithful." Theology, history, and grammar were among the subjects studied. In addition, a separate high school and Hebrew school were conducted in Kirtland during the 1835–36 season. By January 18, 1836, the temple was sufficiently completed for these schools to move into the small rooms on the third floor. Three days later Joseph Smith received the revelation concerning those who died without hearing the gospel; this revelation was added to the Pearl of Great Price in 1976. (*HC*, 2:301, 376, 380.)

These schools were among the earliest adult-education programs in the United States. Unfortunately, however, an increase in persecution interrupted their progress for several years.

Section 89: The Word of Wisdom

According to Brigham Young, this was the first revelation given to the brethren assembled in the School of the Prophets. He described the specific circumstances as follows:

The first school of the prophets was held in a small room situated over the Prophet Joseph's kitchen, in a house which belonged to Bishop Whitney. . . . The brethren came to that place for hundreds of miles to attend school in a little room probably no larger than eleven by fourteen. When they assembled together in this room after breakfast, the first they did was to light their pipes, and, while smoking, talk about the great things of the kingdom, and spit all over the room, and as soon as the pipe was out of their mouths, a large chew of tobacco would then be taken. Often when the Prophet entered the room to give the school instructions he would find himself in a cloud of tobacco smoke. This, and the complaints of his wife at having to clean so filthy a floor, made the Prophet think upon the matter, and he inquired of the Lord relating to the conduct of the Elders in using tobacco, and the revelation known as the Word of Wisdom was the result of his inquiry. (JD, 12:158.)

The widespread temperance movement at the time helped provide a receptive climate for the principles revealed in section 89.

Not by Commandment (Verses 1–3). These verses, which were published as an introduction to this section prior to the 1876 edition, emphasize that the Word of Wisdom was to be received as a revelation of God's will rather than a narrowly restrictive commandment. Perhaps the Lord chose not to make this a binding commandment immediately because this would condemn the brethren without giving them time to overcome their bad habits. Nevertheless, from the beginning the brethren took this principle seriously because it was a revelation and because one should live by all words which come from the mouth of God. (See D&C 84:44.)

Temporal Salvation (Verse 2). Although obeying this revelation brings definite temporal blessings, its main rewards are spiritual as one learns to make his body a worthy temple for the Spirit. Thus, in its most essential aspect this is not a "temporal commandment." (Compare this thought with D&C 29:34.)

Whitney store in Kirtland. Here section 89 was received and the School of the Prophets was held. (Photo courtesy LDS Church archives)

Prohibitions (Verses 5–9). There are two ways of looking at the Word of Wisdom:

1. In a general sense, it is a broad law of health according to which one should avoid anything which is harmful and seek to do anything that will promote one's overall well-being.

2. In the strict sense, the Word of Wisdom is section 89 as officially interpreted by the Church. It is according to the latter interpretation that one's compliance is judged in connection with worthiness for baptism, priesthood advancement, receiving temple recommends, etc. Joseph Smith is quoted as saying that the Lord meant tea and coffee when he said hot drinks. (See Joel Johnson, a close associate of the Prophet's, quoted in John A. and Leah D. Widtsoe's, *The Word of Wisdom,* p. 85.) Brigham Young pointed out that tea and coffee were the common hot drinks at the time this revelation was received. (See *JD,* 12:117–18.) Thus, the four items from which Latter-day Saints should abstain are tobacco, alcohol, tea, and coffee.

Critics have argued that this negative phase of the Word of Wisdom is overstressed. In considering such accusations, one should realize that it is easier to determine compliance or noncompliance if the commandment is specific, such as the prohibitions in this case; perhaps even more important is the fact that the Word of Wisdom is designed for the weakest (verse 3) and so is an appropriate minimum standard.

Positive Aspects (Verses 10–13). The use of fresh fruits, grain, etc., is encouraged. Meat, too, is for the use of man but is to be eaten sparingly. (See verse 12.) Some interpret verse 13 to restrict the use of meat only to periods of cold or famine. Others point out that removing the first comma (absent in the earliest copies of this revelation) would suggest a different meaning—that the Lord was disapproving the idea taught by the Shakers and others that meat should be eaten only in winter. (See discussion about the Shakers' beliefs in connection with section 49 herein.)

Promises (Verses 18–21). As stated above, the benefits arising from keeping this commandment are not only physical but go far beyond. Perhaps the greatest treasure of knowledge which one could ever hope to attain would be the witness that his way of life had prepared him to be exalted in the Lord's kingdom. (For helpful statements made by Church leaders, see Roy W. Doxey, *Latter-day Prophets and the Doctrine and Covenants,* vol. 3, pp. 225–51.)

Section 90: The First Presidency

Because of his faithfulness, Joseph Smith received the promise that the keys of this dispensation would never be taken from him. (See verse 3 and compare this with the conditional promise made earlier; also D&C 43:4.) Two other men were now called to join the Prophet to compose the First Presidency of the Church, which was organized ten days after this revelation was given. Both men had received earlier revelation directing them to work with Joseph Smith: Sidney Rigdon had been told two years earlier to remain with and not forsake the Prophet (D&C 35:22); and just one year before section 90 was given, Frederick G. Williams had been called to be a counselor to Joseph Smith, who held the keys of the Presidency of the High Priesthood (see D&C 81:1–2). Although these brethren were to be equal with Joseph Smith in holding the keys, they would receive the keys and the word of the Lord through the Prophet's administration. (See verses 6–9.) Thus, even though more than one may technically hold the keys, only one man may exercise them actively at a time.

The Lord upheld the Prophet's right to preside not only in Ohio, but in Zion (Missouri), thus refuting rival claims to authority that had arisen in Missouri. (See verses 32–33.) This word was to be sent to the brethren in Missouri in the spirit of love and greeting. (Compare the language in verse 32 with the similar instructions in section 89, verse 2.)

The counsel in verses 25–26 that families should be small had reference, not to the number of children a couple should have, but to the problem of persons unfairly taking advantage of the Saints' hospitality.

Section 91: The Apocrypha

The word *apocryphal* means "of doubtful or questionable origin"; this term is also used to refer in general to noncanonical or nonscriptural writings. "The Apocrypha" is a collection of writings included in Catholic but not in most Protestant Bibles; it comes from the period of Hebrew history roughly between the Old and New Testaments.

The term *apocryphal* should not be confused with *apocalyptic,* which describes a special form of prophetic and highly symbolic Hebrew literature. "The Apocalypse" is the name given to the Revelation of John.

Section 92

The "united order" was a group of top Church leaders whose responsibility it was to administer the law of consecration. (See discussion under section 78 herein.) Because Frederick G. Williams had recently become the second counselor in the First Presidency (D&C 90:6), he was admitted to the order in which he was to be a "lively" (or active) member.

Section 93: The Glory of God

The opening verses of this revelation give the remarkable promise that the faithful will see God's face and behold his glory. The glory of God is the theme which runs throughout the remainder of this great revelation. In verses 7–17, the Lord refers to the testimony of John the Baptist as quoted in the gospel written by the apostle John; the Baptist had the privilege of beholding and bearing witness to Christ's glory.

The Father and the Son (Verses 3–22). Christ might be identified with the Father because he received a fullness of the Father's glory. This might be related to the concept of "divine investiture of authority" as set forth in the First Presidency's statement on "the Father and the Son." (See the discussion of this statement, under section 11 herein. Still, Christ was the "Son" in several senses:

1. Even though he ultimately received of the Father's full-

ness, he did not do so at first, but grew from grace to grace (verses 12–14); similarly, all of God's children who keep his commandments may also know a fullness of God's glory through the grace of Christ (see verses 19–20).

2. Furthermore, Christ was literally the Son of God in two respects: The Only Begotten Son of God in the *flesh* (verse 4), and—

3. the firstborn son of God in the *spirit* (see verse 21). The Lord said that the Father and he were "one"; their oneness consisted in their mutual relationship to the spirit or light of truth. (See the discussion of the unity of the Godhead, p. 49.)

Man's Eternal Intelligence (Verse 29). Chart 13 summarizes the major phases of man's eternal life. Man today might be thought of as a three-stage being: he first existed as *intelligence;* he then became a child of God when his intelligence was clothed in a *spirit* body begotten by his heavenly parents; then, finally, at birth, he received a *physical* body which now houses the inseparable unit of his intelligence and spirit. Verse 29 stresses the fact that the intelligence is eternal, that it never was created but has always existed. In this light, the common phrase "preexistence" is not technically accurate because there is no time before the intelligence existed. It might be more correct to speak of a preearthly or premortal existence.

Chart 13

Man's Eternal Life

First Estate		Second Estate		Third Estate
Preexistence		Probationary State		Four Final States
Intelligence	Spirit	Mortality	Post-Earthly	(Celestial, Terrestrial,
	Unem-bodied	Embodied	Spirit World	Telestial, or Perdition)
			Dis-embodied	Reembodied

Spirit Birth | Physical Birth | Death | Resurrection and Judgment

Independence and Agency (Verses 30–31). Section 93 may help Latter-day Saints understand the origin of evil. The traditional Christian view holds that God "created" everything *ex nihilo* (out of nothing) and, therefore, that he must be responsible for everything that exists, good or evil. In contrast to this notion, section 93 affirms that at least two things, intelligence and material elements, have always existed and, therefore, that God is not necessarily responsible for evil that might come from those sources. On a more positive note, man's eternal intelligence may be the ultimate source of his free agency. (See verse 31.) The exact nature of the intelligence is not known, but the fact that this subject was presented by the Lord in the midst of his discussion of glory, truth, and light may suggest that these are essential qualities of man's eternal intelligence.

"The Glory of God Is Intelligence" (Verse 36). The term *intelligence* may be understood in two rather distinct senses: (1) Commonly, it refers to mental ability or the capacity to learn and reason. (2) Latter-day Saints identify "intelligence" with that portion of our being which is eternal or uncreated. One must read the context in order to determine which of these senses is intended in verse 36.

Notice how the words used in verse 36 to describe God's glory are also found in verse 29 in reference to man's condition in the beginning. God the Father possesses these powers and attributes in full. Although the Son did not have a fullness at first, he progressed to the point that he did receive a fullness of the Father's glory. (Verses 12–16.) Verse 19 may be regarded as setting forth the basic thesis of section 93— that through Jesus Christ, men also may attain a fullness of the Father's glory. This may be accomplished through obedience to the Lord's commandments. (Contrast verses 27–28 with verse 39.)

Thus "intelligence" in verse 36 should be understood in a broader spiritual sense rather than only in its strictly academic meaning. Physical *light* has often been emphasized in descriptions of the glory possessed by heavenly messengers. (Consider, for example, Joseph Smith's accounts of the Father and the Son and of the angel Moroni.) Light is also intertwined with the powers of God's Spirit. (See the discussion of the Spirit or Light of Christ on p. 131.) "Intelligence" in D&C 130:18–19 should likewise be understood in this enlarged sense. Similarly, the declaration in D&C 131:6 that "it is impossible for a man to be saved in ignorance" takes on an essentially spiritual meaning when read in the context of the preceding verse.

Even though these passages should be understood in a broader and primarily spiritual sense, "intelligence" being developed primarily through righteous obedience, secular study and learning are not excluded. *Truth,* which is one of the key ingredients of intelligence and God's glory, is defined in verse 24 as *"knowledge* of things as they are, and as they were, and as they are to be" (italics added). Perhaps the strongest scriptural basis for the Church's interest in education is to be found in section 88. (See the discussion of D&C 88:76–80 herein.)

Sections 94–96: The Building Up of Kirtland

During the spring of 1833, the brethren were concerned with the building up of the city of Kirtland. These three revelations were given at that time to explain various phases of the work. Section 95 encouraged Church members to respond favorably to the appeal for funds to build the temple. Section 96 settled a disagreement by assigning the bishop to take charge of certain properties held by the Church in Kirtland.

Three Important Buildings. During the previous December, the Lord had directed the erection of the Kirtland Temple. (See D&C 88:119.) Now, however, the brethren were giving more attention to the erection of two other buildings, a "house for the presidency" and a printing establishment, to be located respectively on the first and second lots south of the temple, each building having upper and lower rooms measuring 55 by 65 feet. (See D&C 94:3–12.) Even though the Lord approved these plans, the buildings were not to be erected until he gave further commandments concerning them. (See D&C 94:16.)

Section 95 directed the elders' attention again to the temple, which was the most important building they should construct. The temple was to be built following the same general pattern as the two buildings above, the lower room being devoted to sacrament, fast, and other worship meetings, and the upper room being used for the "school of mine apostles." (D&C 95:13–17.)

Several uses and purposes of the temple were suggested in these revelations. The apostles were to be prepared for their ministry by receiving an endowment of power from on high. (See D&C 95:4, 8.)

The Lord's "Strange Act" (D&C 95:1–4). The phrase "strange act" apparently is an allusion to Isaiah 28:21. To the world, for example, it may seem strange for the Lord to chasten and rebuke those whom he loves; nevertheless, this is done for their own good.

Section 97: Difficulties in Jackson County

This revelation came exactly two years after the land of Zion had been dedicated in 1831. During this period many Latter-day Saints had gathered to the area, but unfortunately they experienced antagonisms with their non-Mormon neighbors.

For several months tensions between Mormons and non-Mormons grew in Jackson County, Missouri, culminating in the destruction of the Latter-day Saints' press on July 20, 1833. It was in this attack that most of the copies of the newly completed Book of Commandments were lost.

Some of the causes of this friction included the following:

1. The Latter-day Saints belonged to what was thought of as a strange religion, and their cultural background was not the same as that of the majority.

2. The 1820 Missouri Compromise had made Missouri a slave state, while the Latter-day Saints had come from the antislave North.

3. By 1833 there were enough Mormons to fairly well dominate Jackson County politics and wield quite an influence throughout the state as well.

4. Some of the Saints lacked good judgment and boasted

that Jackson County was their Zion by divine decree.

These and other factors antagonized the earlier settlers in the area. Because the lawless element tended to flock to the frontier, these antagonisms resulted in mob violence against the Saints.

As difficulties mounted during the early summer of 1833, word was sent to Joseph Smith in Kirtland, and it was in this setting that sections 97 and 98 were given.

A Temple in Zion (Verses 10–17). Location of the Independence, Jackson County, Missouri, temple had been revealed two years earlier. (See D&C 57:3.) Recently discovered preliminary sketches for this temple indicate that it would have been built "like unto the pattern" which the Lord had given for the Kirtland Temple. (See D&C 97:10.)

The temple would have been a source of temporal as well as spiritual salvation for the Saints in Zion. By means of a parable in a subsequent revelation, the Lord spoke of his servants' failure to build a tower (or the temple) as he had commanded in order to provide defense. (See D&C 101:43–62.)

In section 97, verses 13 and 14 list functions of temples, and verses 15–17 set forth a marvelous promise which may be applied to these sacred structures today as well as to the contemplated temple in Zion.

Warning to the Saints in Zion (Verses 18–26). According to verse 21, *Zion* refers to the "pure in heart." Thus, the Lord was pleased with the humble, righteous Saints in Missouri; but at the same time, he chastened those in need of repentance. The Lord stressed that righteous Zion would be protected during the time when scourges would be swept over the wicked. Nevertheless, if the inhabitants of Zion failed to keep the Lord's commandments, she, too, would partake of the afflictions to come upon the disobedient. In the light of immediate future events, this was a very timely warning.

Section 98

Each of the major teachings in this section can be related to the pending violence in Jackson County. (For a review

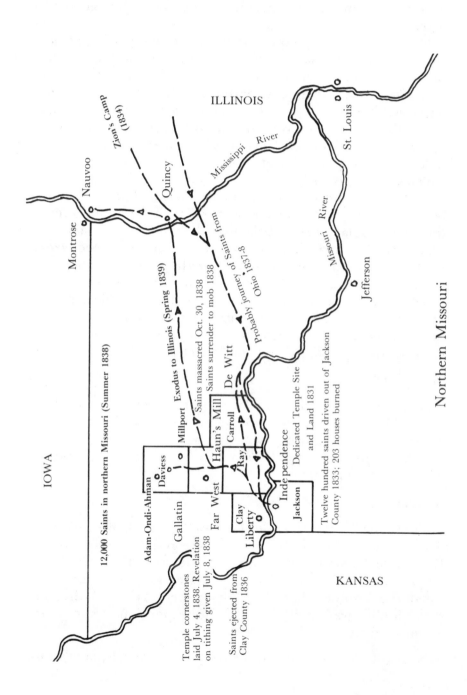

ILLINOIS

Zion's Camp (1834)

Nauvoo

Montrose

Quincy

Mississippi   River

St. Louis

Missouri   River

Jefferson

IOWA

12,000 Saints in northern Missouri (Summer 1838)

Millport   Exodus to Illinois (Spring 1839)

Saints massacred Oct. 30, 1838

Saints surrender to mob 1838

Probably journey of Saints from Ohio 1837-8

De Witt

Adam-Ondi-Ahman

Daviess

Gallatin

Haun's Mill

Carroll

Far West

Ray

Clay

Liberty

Independence   Dedicated Temple Site and Land 1831

Jackson

Twelve hundred saints driven out of Jackson County 1833; 203 houses burned

Temple cornerstones laid July 4, 1838. Revelation on tithing given July 8, 1838

Saints ejected from Clay County 1836

KANSAS

Northern Missouri

of these circumstances, see the discussion under section 97 herein.)

In verses 4–10, the Lord reminded the Saints of their obligation to sustain the Constitutional law of the land despite the crises of mob persecution. (See the discussion under section 134 herein for a consideration of the Latter-day Saints' responsibility to civil law. The Saints knew from bitter experience that "when the wicked rule, the people mourn" (verse 9), so the Lord counseled his people to take positive steps to seek and uphold good men rather than resorting to further violence (see verse 10).

Latter-day Saints were not to be afraid of their enemies, because these afflictions were to prove their faith, and even if they had to lay down their lives for the Lord's sake, the righteous still had the promise of eternal life. (See verses 11–15.) Verse 16 contains what is perhaps the key theme in section 98—that above all, the Saints were to work for peace.

There were opportunities almost daily to implement the instructions in verses 23–48 concerning forgiving and not retaliating against one's enemies who do or do not repent. (See the discussion on forgiveness under section 64 herein.)

Section 99

John Murdock's wife had died shortly after giving birth to twins. These babies were later adopted by Joseph and Emma Smith, who had just lost twins of their own. Elder Murdock remained faithful in the Church, serving as a bishop both in Missouri and in Nauvoo.

Section 100

The Saints' difficulties in Jackson County continued during the fall of 1833. Before leaving on his mission to the East, Joseph Smith sent Orson Hyde and John Gould to check on conditions in Missouri. In section 100 the Lord assured the Prophet that these elders were safe and that his own family was well and gave the missionaries encouragement in their work.

Sidney Rigdon as Spokesman (Verses 9–11). Sidney Rigdon's former experience as a minister prepared him well for his new calling as Joseph Smith's spokesman. He had also served as the Prophet's scribe (section 35) and more recently had been called as his first counselor (D&C 90:6). Elder Rigdon's new calling was put in proper perspective when the Lord reminded him that Joseph Smith would still be the revelator. Thus Joseph and Sidney served in the same relative positions as had Moses and Aaron anciently.

Section 101

Mob violence in Jackson County continued until the Saints were forced to evacuate the area in November 1833. (See comments under section 97 herein.) It was with the background of this extreme suffering that section 101 was received.

Cause of the Saints' Suffering (Verses 1–9). The Saints' own failings were to blame for their suffering. Their transgressions, disunity, lustfulness, and slowness in hearkening to the Lord were in marked contrast to the ideals which must characterize a Zion people—unity and righteousness. (See, for example, D&C 97:21–26 and Moses 7:18.) The Saints needed further chastening and purifying, and the Lord promised he would be merciful toward them.

Two Phases of Gathering (Verses 17–22). Despite the Saints' difficulties, the appointed place of gathering would not be changed. Nevertheless, a time would come when there would be no more gathering to one central location and when other gathering places would be designated. These two phases of gathering have been reflected in Church history: (1) During most of the nineteenth century, Latter-day Saint converts gathered to the Rocky Mountains. (2) During the twentieth century, Church leaders have counseled the Saints to remain in their own lands and to build up the kingdom there. Hundreds of "stakes of Zion" have been set up around the world. Like the city of Zion itself, these stakes are to be places of refuge amid latter-day tribulations. (Compare D&C 115:5–6, 17–18.)

The Millennium (Verses 24–34)

In the midst of these difficulties, the Lord explained that his Saints should gather in preparation for glorious events, especially those associated with the inauguration of his Millennial reign on earth. One of the major purposes of this special thousand-year period is to make it possible for all of God's children to prove themselves and to receive necessary ordinances. For this reason, temple work will be accelerated during the Millennium.

Earth to Be Changed (Verses 24–25). These verses refer to the earth being cleansed by fire and being raised from its present telestial state to a higher terrestrial condition at the beginning of the Millennium. (See the discussion and chart of the history of the earth under section 77 herein.)

Satan to Be Bound (Verse 28). Satan will not be able to tempt inhabitants of the earth during the Millennium because of: (1) the righteousness of the people (1 Ne. 22:26); (2) the power of Jesus Christ, who will be reigning personally on the earth; and (3) the fact that the earth itself will have been elevated to a higher plane further removed from Satan's realm.

Life and Death during the Millennium (Verses 29–31). Those who are worthy of the celestial kingdom will be "quickened and be caught up to meet" Christ in the clouds of heaven and then descend with him in his coming in glory. (See D&C 88:96.) Those worthy of the terrestrial kingdom will be "quickened but not caught up." The "quickening" refers to the individual's being changed (like the earth) from a telestial to terrestrial mortal state. (See Chart 3 under section 7 herein.) Those living only on a telestial level or lower will not be worthy to remain on earth in its terrestrial condition, so they will be burned as stubble. (See Malachi 4:1.)

Those who are alive when the Millennium begins or who are born during the thousand years will live in a terrestrial mortal state until they reach the "age of a tree" (verses 29–31), "the age of man" (D&C 63:49–50), or, as Isaiah specified, the age of 100 years (see Isaiah 65:20). At that point they will be "changed in a twinkling of an eye," or, in other words, pass through a change equal to death and an instantaneous resurrection to an immortal state, either celestial or terrestrial depending on the individual's worthiness. Thus, during the Millennium, there will be a step equal to death, but there will be no death as we know it in that none will sleep, "that is to say in the earth." (Verses 29-31). (For Joseph Fielding Smith's discussion of the Millennium, see *Doctrines of Salvation,* vol. 3, chap. 4.)

Instructions through Parables (Verses 42-101)

Parable of the Vineyard (Verses 43-62). A certain nobleman (the Lord Jesus Christ) commanded his servants to go and plant a vineyard (establish Zion) on a choice piece of ground (the American continent). The servants were to erect a tower, the temple (compare D&C 97:12), as a means to see their enemies while they were still far away and thereby still had time to defend themselves (received by revelation in the temple—the Lord's warning for the future). The servants failed to build the tower as commanded, so when the enemies came the servants were scattered and the vineyard was destroyed. The Lord then directed another servant, Joseph Smith (see D&C 103:21), to take the strong and young from among his servants (Zion's Camp) and drive the enemy out of the vineyard. Then "by and by" (verse 58), "after many days" (verse 62), the Lord and his people would again possess the land and all things would be fulfilled.

Wheat and Tares (Verses 64-75). The parable of the good wheat being gathered and the tares being burned was compared to the righteous gathering of the Saints. In connection with this gathering, the Lord directed his people to continue purchasing land in and around Jackson County and not to sell what they already possessed there. (See also verses 96-101. See discussion of this parable under section 86 herein.)

Importunate Widow (Verses 76-89). The Saints were to continue importuning or petitioning government officials for redress even as did the widow in this parable. While introducing this counsel, the Lord revealed the significant fact that he had established the Constitution of the United States "by the hands of wise men whom I raised up unto this very purpose." (Verse 80.) (See discussion under section 134 herein on Latter-day Saints' responsibility on civil law.)

Section 102: The First High Council

This section is unique in that it consists of an extract from the minutes of the meeting in which the first high council in the Church was organized. This event marks the formal beginning of the Kirtland Stake, the first stake in the Church.

This particular high council had powers not generally exercised by such councils in the Church today. (See verses 26–27.) It was unique in that its presidency was the First Presidency of the Church; for a time it was the only high council, no other "standing" high council or the "traveling high council" (Council of the Twelve Apostles) yet being in existence.

High councils have "semi-administrative" as well as judicial functions. (For an excellent discussion on Church administration, see Elder Harold B. Lee's talk and charts in the *Church News*, August 26, 1961, pp. 8–15.) Section 102 concentrates on the high council's judicial function.

Judicial Structure of the Church

"Priesthood courts of the Church are not courts of retribution," declared Bishop Robert L. Simpson, "they are courts of love." Their purpose is to help the transgressor to take "the first giant step back." (*CR*, April 1972, pp. 31–33.)

Ward Bishop's Court. This is the first of the three "regular courts." (See D&C 107:72–75.) This court has "original jurisdiction" in most matters. It may disfellowship anyone found guilty of sufficiently serious violation of Church standards; a person so penalized retains his membership and priesthood but is forbidden to take an active part in the Church. The bishop's court may excommunicate anyone except a bearer of the Melchizedek Priesthood; this penalty actually removes a person from membership in the Church, making it necessary for him to reenter by baptism when he repents.

Stake High Council. This court handles matters beyond the scope of the ward bishop (D&C 102:2) and may hear appeals from the bishop's court. Section 102 (verses 12–23) outlines the procedures followed by this council when sitting as a judicial body.

First Presidency Court. This is the "regular court" having final jurisdiction in all matters. (See D&C 107:78–81.) This court was given the specific responsibility of trying a Presiding Bishop in case of the latter's transgression. (See D&C 68:22–24.)

Special Courts. There are three "special courts" mentioned in the Doctrine and Covenants:

1. A council of high priests abroad may be called to consider the most serious matters. (D&C 102:28–29.)

2. The traveling high council composed of the Twelve Apostles constitutes a special court from which there is no appeal (D&C 102:30–31), although the apostles may be tried by the "general authorities" in case of transgression. (See verse 32. Note that this is the first use in the Doctrine and Covenants of the phase "general authorities.") Both of these courts were designed to handle matters arising outside of the geographical jurisdiction of regular courts; but, with the development of mission organizations, there is not so much need today for these special courts.

3. The Presiding Bishopric, assisted by twelve high priests, may try members of the First Presidency in case of transgression. (D&C 107:82–83; for additional information, see John A. Widtsoe, *Priesthood and Church Government,* chap. 17.)

Section 103 and Zion's Camp

In the opening verses of this revelation the Lord again commented on the cause of the Saints' difficulties. (Compare sections 101 and 105.) He had respected the agency even of the wicked, allowing them to "fill up the measure of their iniquities." Nevertheless, this "sore and grievous chastisement" had come upon the Saints because of their own failure to keep the commandments. (See verses 2-4.)

The governor of Missouri had suggested that the Latter-day Saints raise a force to work with the state militia in restoring the exiled Mormons to their homes in Jackson County. Section 103, given in February 1834, directed the Saints to raise such a force from among the strength of the Church. This group, known as "Zion's Camp," left Kirtland during May and arrived in Missouri in June 1834. Along the way the Kirtland contingent was supplemented by volunteers from other areas, bringing the total to 205 men. Purposes of Zion's Camp also included taking provisions for the relief of the exiles who had by that time settled in Clay County.

Section 104: Economic Affairs

Two basic developments in Church economic structure were reflected in this revelation:

1. About two weeks before this revelation was given, the law of consecration was suspended in Kirtland so that "the innocent among you may not be condemned with the unjust." (Verse 7.) Verses 19-46 discuss the disposition of property which had belonged to the order. Nevertheless, the principle of stewardship was maintained; the Lord reminded the brethren that all things belonged to him and that they were stewards accountable to him. (See verses 11-13, 55-57.) Two treasuries were to be established—one a sacred treasury (verses 60-66), and the other a treasury from which faithful members could obtain financial help when needed (see verses 67-77).

2. The "united order," or administrative body for economic affairs (see discussion under sections 42 and 78 herein) was to be divided—one group over affairs at Kirtland and the other over affairs in Missouri. If both areas had remained one economic unit, all would have been weakened by the Missouri persecutions; this move to separate them would allow Kirtland to remain strong and thus be in a better position to assist the Saints in Zion. Furthermore, because of the suspension of consecration in Ohio and because of the prob-

lems related to the persecutions in Missouri, the two areas were in different economic circumstances.

Section 105: Requirements for Redeeming Zion

Members of Zion's Camp arrived in Missouri in June 1834. They learned that the governor, who was anxious to avoid bloodshed and to find a peaceful solution, had withdrawn his offer to use the state militia to help the Saints. The Lord revealed section 105 at this point to instruct the members of Zion's Camp as well as the Saints residing in Missouri concerning their future course.

Why had the brethren failed to achieve their immediate goal of being restored to their land in Zion? The Lord enumerated several reasons. (Compare verses 1-9 with D&C 101:1-8; 103:1-14.) The transgressions of the Saints themselves were at the heart of the problem; they were not united and had failed to impart of their substance to the poor by means of living the law of consecration. (D&C 105:3-5.) They had been slow in responding to the Lord's commandments. (D&C 101:7-8.) Therefore, the people had to be chastened until they learned more perfect obedience. (D&C 105:6.)

Concerning the future, the Lord wisely counseled his people not to boast of judgments, etc., but to consider the feelings of others regarding the gathering of the Saints. (D&C 105:24.) The elders were to continue purchasing land in the area, but the redemption of Zion had to wait until the Lord's people themselves were prepared (verse 10), had become more numerous and "sanctified" or worthy (verse 31), and had received an endowment of power from on high in the Kirtland Temple (verses 11-12, 33). The Lord explained that the fulfillment of the various commandments and promises concerning Zion would have to await the redemption of the land. (Verses 9 and 34.)

Did Zion's Camp accomplish anything? Even though the immediate objective was not realized, this experience demonstrated the faith and devotion of several future Church leaders. During the march, Joseph Smith had the opportunity to become better acquainted with these men. The original Twelve Apostles and First Quorum of the Seventy were first chosen from among those who had responded to the call to join Zion's Camp. This lengthy cross-country march provided valuable experience to Church leaders who later had to direct the forced evacuation of men, women, and children under much more difficult circumstances.

Section 106

Warren A. Cowdery (the brother of Oliver Cowdery) was to preside over the branch in Freedom, New York. His assignment to prepare for the Lord's second coming is still among the important objectives of the Church's programs today.

Section 107: Revelation on Priesthood

Both sections 84 and 107 have been designated "Revelation on Priesthood." The first apostles and seventies in the Church had been called in February 1835; this revelation was given to explain the responsibilities of these and other offices in the Church.

Section 107 is a composite of at least two major revelations. Verses 1–58 were dated March 1835. Notice how verse 58 introduces a separate revelation which had been received earlier; the earliest known manuscript of this portion of section 107 is dated November 1831. The earlier revelation did not include verses 93–98; the date of this "vision showing the order of the Seventy" (verse 93) is not known, but it must have been received before that quorum was organized in February 1835.

For convenience of study, section 107 may be divided as follows: (1) history and orders of the priesthood—verses 1–20, 40–57; (2) presiding quorums—verses 21–39; and (3) other priesthood offices and quorums—verses 58–100.

Priesthood History and Orders (Verses 1–20, 40–57)

The first mortal placed on earth was the man Adam, one of God's choicest spirit offspring and a leader in the councils and other activities of our preearthly existence. The scrip-

Chart 14
Apostasy and Restoration

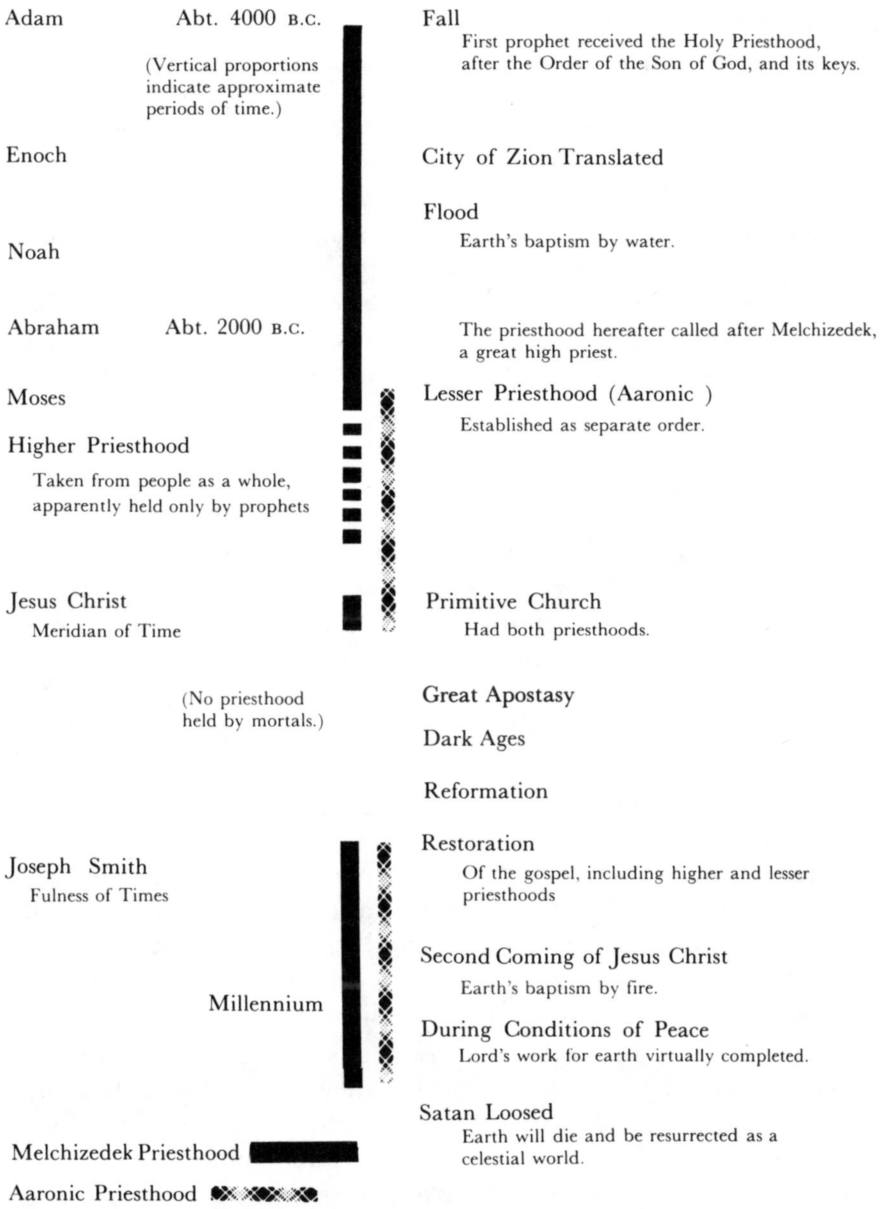

Adam   Abt. 4000 B.C.

(Vertical proportions indicate approximate periods of time.)

Enoch

Noah

Abraham   Abt. 2000 B.C.

Moses

Higher Priesthood

Taken from people as a whole, apparently held only by prophets

Jesus Christ
Meridian of Time

(No priesthood held by mortals.)

Joseph Smith
Fulness of Times

Millennium

Melchizedek Priesthood

Aaronic Priesthood

Fall
First prophet received the Holy Priesthood, after the Order of the Son of God, and its keys.

City of Zion Translated

Flood
Earth's baptism by water.

The priesthood hereafter called after Melchizedek, a great high priest.

Lesser Priesthood (Aaronic)
Established as separate order.

Primitive Church
Had both priesthoods.

Great Apostasy

Dark Ages

Reformation

Restoration
Of the gospel, including higher and lesser priesthoods

Second Coming of Jesus Christ
Earth's baptism by fire.

During Conditions of Peace
Lord's work for earth virtually completed.

Satan Loosed
Earth will die and be resurrected as a celestial world.

tures indicate that it was not good that Adam should be alone, so the Lord created Eve to be a companion for him. Our first parents had a numerous posterity, and, as parents always should, they taught their children the commandments of God.

Adam had direct and personal contact with the Lord while in the Garden of Eden, but even after his expulsion because of transgression, Adam continued to receive revelations from God.

Adam functioned as God's spokesman, receiving revelation from the Lord and, in turn, declaring his word to the people. Men who function in such a capacity are known as prophets. The word *prophet* refers to one who speaks for another; in this case, *prophet* refers to one who speaks for God. Thus, Adam was not only the first man on earth, but he was also the first prophet of God.

Because God is a God of order, those who minister for him on earth must do so by his authority or priesthood. As a prophet, Adam held the priesthood. The authority was the same as that which we know today as the Melchizedek Priesthood. The Doctrine and Covenants states that in the days of Adam this authority was known as "the Holy Priesthood, after the Order of the Son of God." (D&C 107:3; see Chart 14.)

The force of God's revelation and inspiration given through the prophets has always been opposed by the force of evil coming into the world via Satan's temptations. During the days of Adam, Satan was successful in leading astray a part of Adam's posterity. The scriptures refer to such a falling away into darkness as an "apostasy"—a Greek word whose components mean "to stand away." In ancient literature, this word *apostasy* was used to describe rebellions in which rightful leadership was overthrown illegally.

Because one of God's purposes in sending his children to the earth was to see how faithful they would be in keeping his commandments, it was not pleasing to him that they should remain in a state of darkness and ignorance. For this reason, he has always sent prophets to "restore" men to a knowledge of his word. These acts of sending the gospel to the earth again are called "dispensations" because the Lord's word and power are dispensed or sent forth from heaven. The term *dispensation* may also refer to the period of time which elapses from one restoration to another, and generally bears the name of the prophet who stood at its head. Hence, the first of these periods was the "Dispensation of Adam."

The prophet whom the Lord chose to head the second dispensation was Enoch, who is remembered most for the tremendous work he did in converting the entire city of Zion so thoroughly that it was taken into heaven because of righteousness. Satan again gained influence over those who remained behind, and a second apostasy followed.

Priesthood Lineage (Verses 41–52). On the surface there appears to be a discrepancy between this lineage and that given in D&C 84:6–16. The former traced the priesthood through Seth, and the latter through Abel. This apparent problem is resolved when one realizes that Seth was appointed to take the place of the slain Abel in terms of posterity and priesthood blessings. (See Moses 6:2).

Chart 15
The Early Patriarchs

Name	Year Born*	Year Ordained*	Age	By Whom	Year Died	Age
Adam					930	930
Seth	130	199	69	Adam	1142	912
Enos	235	369	134	Adam	1140	905
Cainan	325	412	87	Adam	1235	910
Mahalaleel	395	891	496	Adam	1290	895
Jared	460	660	200	Adam	1422	962
Enoch	622	647	25	Adam	1052	430**
Methuselah	687	787	100	Adam	1656	969
Lamech	874	906	32	Seth	1651	777
Noah	1056	1066	10	Methuselah	2006	950

*Years are numbered from Adam's fall. One can approximate the date of this event as 4000 B.C. and thereby convert the years shown on the chart into dates before Christ.

**Date of translation, not death. (Moses 6:10-25; 7:68-8:12; Genesis 5; D&C 107:41-52.)

The Lord again followed his pattern of sending a prophet to take the people from spiritual darkness. The third great prophet was Noah, who preached for 120 years but with little success. The people were so wicked that only Noah's immediate family accepted his message. Thus, when the floods came, only eight were saved in the ark. (See 1 Peter 3:18–20.) For a time, Noah's family lived in righteousness, but eventually the people again fell into apostasy.

Name of Priesthood Changed (Verses 2–4.) The prophet sent to head the restoration in the fourth dispensation was Abraham, the father of God's covenant people. Like his predecessors, Abraham held the priesthood, having been ordained by another great man of his day, Melchizedek, a high priest of God and the king of Salem. (See D&C 84:14.) It was during Abraham's day that the name of the priesthood was changed to the Melchizedek Priesthood. This was done in order to avoid the too frequent mention of Deity. Although it had a new name, this was the same priesthood which Adam, Enoch, and Noah possessed.

Two Orders of Priesthood. Following a period of physical bondage in Egypt and a time of spiritual apostasy, God sent Moses to head the fifth great dispensation. As a prophet, Moses held the higher priesthood. His older brother Aaron was appointed to assist him and was given a lesser priesthood which became known as the Priesthood of Aaron. Section 107 explains the relationship which exists between these two orders of priesthood.

The Melchizedek and Aaronic Priesthoods. The Aaronic Priesthood may be regarded as "lesser" because it deals with temporal things, because it administers the outward ordinances pertaining to the "preparatory gospel" (which prepares the individual to receive greater spiritual blessings), and because it is an appendage to the greater priesthood. (Compare verses 13–14 and 20 with D&C 13 and D&C 84:26–27.) The Melchizedek Priesthood, on the other hand, has the right of presidency and administers spiritual things; through the authority and ordinances of this priesthood, the power of God is manifested. By this same authority, a person may receive the "mysteries of the kingdom" or the knowledge of God (see discussion on mysteries under section 6 herein) which prepares the individual to have the heavens opened to him and to enjoy communion with the Father and the Son. (Compare verses 18–19 with D&C 84:19-22.)

Lesser: Aaronic	Greater: Melchizedek
Appendage to greater priesthood (D&C 107:14)	All other authorities are appendages; presidency over all other offices (D&C 107:5, 8)
Administers temporal affairs (D&C 107:68)	Administers in spiritual things (D&C 107:8)
"Preparatory gospel" of repentance and baptism (D&C section 13; 84:26-27)	Holds keys to spiritual blessings (D&C 107:18)
"Outward ordinances" (D&C 107:14, 20)	
"Justification" (D&C 20:30)	"Sanctification" (D&C 20:31)
Ministry of angels (D&C Sections 13; 84:26; 107:20)	Keys of the "mysteries of godliness" and of seeing and communing with God (D&C 84:19-22; 107:19.)

Aaronic vs. Levitical Priesthood. Because of the people's hardheartedness, the Melchizedek Priesthood was withdrawn from Israel following the time of Moses. Although a few prophets were especially ordained to the higher priesthood, section 84 states that only the Aaronic Priesthood was passed down through the Israelite nation as a whole.

Because members of the tribe of Levi were assigned to serve in the Lesser Priesthood, this authority also became known as the Levitical Priesthood. Hence "Aaronic Priesthood" and "Levitical Priesthood" are two names for the same lesser order. (See D&C 107:6.) All who bore this priesthood were called "priests" in the Old Testament. Nevertheless, the direct descendants of Aaron were called to preside, as do bishops in our dispensation. The rest of the

Levites were presided over, and they were assigned to the more menial tasks which may correspond to the functions of present-day teachers and deacons. Thus, all held the same lesser priesthood, but the authority of the descendants of Aaron was greater and included that which was given to the Levites in general. (See D&C 107:1.) As the centuries passed, another period of spiritual darkness came over Israel, and even most of the Aaronic priests became corrupted. (See D&C 84:23-28.)

Later Dispensations. The sixth dispensation is known as the dispensation of the meridian of times because it stood at about the midway point in the history of the world and because the birth of Christ is the point from which years before and after are numbered. This time God sent more than a prophet; he sent his Only Begotten Son in the flesh, Jesus Christ. The Savior restored a knowledge of the gospel to mankind and organized a church in which both the Melchizedek and Aaronic priesthoods were again found on the earth. (See Hebrews 7:11.) Following the death of Christ's apostles, the greatest of all the apostasies fell over the earth.

In our own day, the Lord opened the dispensation of the fullness of times by following the pattern which was by now well established—sending a prophet through whom he could restore to the people a knowledge of the gospel. The Doctrine and Covenants is, in a very real sense, the primary history of the revelations through which the priesthood, Church, and basic gospel doctrines have been restored. (For a review of the history of the priesthood on earth, see John A. Widstoe, *Priesthood and Church Government,* chap. 1.)

Presiding Quorums (Verses 21-39)

The general administration of the Church is based on quorums. Section 107 speaks of the First Presidency, the Council of the Twelve Apostles, and the First Quorum of the Seventy as being "equal in authority." (Verses 22-38.) This means they are *potentially* equal, but the revelation is clear in pointing out that the Twelve work under the direction of the First

Presidency and that the Seventy, in turn, labor under the Twelve.

Quorum of the First Presidency (Verse 22). The president of this quorum stands at the head of the priesthood structure and is known as the presiding high priest or President of the High Priesthood. As head of the ecclesiastical structure he is called the president of the Church. He holds the keys of spiritual blessings and may officiate in all other offices in the Church. He possesses gifts enabling him to be a prophet, seer, revelator, and translator; and he holds the keys to all spiritual blessings. (See verses 9, 65–67, and 91–92, and D&C 21:1.) The Quorum of the First Presidency is composed of three presiding high priests, although Joseph Smith and Brigham Young for a time had five "assistant counselors." David O. McKay also expanded the quorum by calling additional "counselors" who were distinguished from the original two counselors by not having a number (first counselor, second counselor, etc.) assigned them.

Even though only a simple majority is generally necessary for a quorum to function, the Quorum of the First Presidency is dissolved with the death of the president because the counselors are set apart as counselors to the particular president; with his death they are automatically released. The remaining members of the First Presidency then return to their former quorums—often, but not always, the Quorum of the Twelve.

Council of the Twelve Apostles. In addition to being special witnesses, members of this quorum work under the direction of the First Presidency in building up the Lord's kingdom and regulating and setting in order the various officers thereof. In this capacity the quorum is called a "traveling, presiding high council" in distinction to the local stake councils which are called "standing high councils." (See verses 33 and 38.)

When the First Presidency is dissolved, the Council of the Twelve automatically becomes the presiding quorum and its senior member the presiding officer of the Church. President Wilford Woodruff taught that this pattern was inspired; it brings to the presidency of the Church the man who has the longest experience in the Quorum of the Twelve. (See Matthias Cowley, *Wilford Woodruff*, p. 561.)

The First Quorum of the Seventy (Verses 25-26). When the initial quorum of the seventy was called in 1835, only its seven presidents were regarded as General Authorities. By the mid 1840s, several other quorums of seventy had been organized, and their presidents became members of the "first quorum" and were presided over by the presidents of this quorum, who were known as "The First Council of the Seventy." After the Pioneers' exodus to the West, the number of seventies quorums multiplied greatly, and they were scattered from Canada to Mexico. Under these conditions only the seven presidents of the first quorum continued to function as a distinct body. By 1975, however, more help was needed to administer the worldwide Church. For the first time, additional members, who were to be General Authorities, were added to the First Quorum of the Seventy. By the following year, the combined total of Assistants to the Twelve and of members of the First Quorum of the Seventy exceeded 36, the minimum required to organize a Church-level seventies quorum (because it represents a majority of the total 70); at this time the First Quorum of the Seventy was formally organized and included the Assistants to the Twelve as members.

This is the third quorum which is "equal in authority" with the Twelve and the First Presidency. The seventies were now in a better position to provide the assistance to the Twelve as called for in verse 38. Note the similarity of the assignments given to these two quorums as reflected in the following verses from section 107:

Twelve	Seventy
23. Apostles to be special witnesses.	25. To preach and be especial witnesses.
24. Quorum equal in authority to the First Presidency.	26. Quorum equal in authority to the Twelve.
33. Under direction of the Presidency, build up and regulate the Church in all nations.	34. Under direction of the Twelve, build up and regulate the Church in all nations.

See also similar instructions given to the New Testament Twelve (Matthew 9:37 to 10:23) and Seventy (Luke 10:1-12, 17-20)

Other Presiding Quorums (Verses 36-37). At the time section 107 was revealed, there were only two stake high councils in the Church. Elder John Taylor later explained that they had unusual powers not generally accorded to such bodies. The high council in Kirtland, for example, was unique in that it was headed by the First Presidency of the Church. (*JD,* 19:241.)

Priesthood Offices

There are nine priesthood offices which one receives by being "ordained." (See Chart 16.) These are permanent in that they are never lost except through excommunication. Of course, if a person becomes unworthy to bear the priesthood, it ceases to be a source of personal blessing to him. (See D&C 121:37.) Thus, the saying "once a bishop always a bishop," is true, and the same principle also applies to all the offices discussed below. In contrast to these priesthood offices, ecclesiastical offices (such as stake president, quorum president, auxiliary officer, etc.) which one receives by being "set apart," are not permanent because it is customary to release such officers following a period of service. The Lord has explained that these officers are necessary so that someone may hold the keys, or, in other words, direct the work of other priesthood bearers in the Church. (See D&C 124:123, 143.) For example, the President of the High Priesthood is set apart to preside over the whole Church and has the calling to serve as prophet, seer, revelator, etc. (See verses 65-67, 91-92; D&C 124:125.)

Apostle. This office in the priesthood has the power to establish the kingdom of God throughout the earth—the apostles being called as special witnesses of the name of Christ in all the world. (Verses 23, 58.)

Patriarch. "Evangelical ministers" or "evangelists," as patriarchs are also called, hold the keys of sealing blessings upon the faithful. (Verse 39 and footnote. See also D&C 124:124.) The word *evangel* means "gospel"; thus, a patriarchal blessing is an inspired application of specific teachings and promises

Chart 16
Priesthood Offices

Office	Functions	Quorums	Restored	References
Aaronic Priesthood restored by John the Baptist, May 15, 1829 (Doctrine and Covenants 13; *History of the Church*, vol. 1, pages 39, 40)				
Deacon	To warn and teach; temporal duties (20:59)	12 deacons (107:85)	1830	1 Timothy 3:8-13
Teacher	To watch over the Church always (20:53-58)	24 teachers (107:86)	1830	Ephesians 4:11 1 Corinthians 12:28
Priest	To preach, teach, expound, baptize, administer sacrament, and ordain (20:46-52)	48 priests (107:87-88); bishop is president of quorum	1830	Hebrews 10:11 Acts 6:7
Bishop	"A judge in Israel"(58:16-18; 107:72-74); to administer in temporal affairs (107:68)		February 4, 1831 (see section 41)	1 Timothy 3:1-7 Titus 1:7-9

Melchizedek Priesthood restored between May 15 and June 30, 1829 (*History of the Church*, vol. 1, pages 40-42)

Office	Duties	Date	Scriptures
Elder	A standing minister (124:137); to administer in spiritual things (107:12), ordain, lay on hands to bestow Holy Ghost, conduct meetings (20:38-45)	96 elders (107:89)	April 6, 1830	Acts 14:23 / James 5:14 / 1 Peter 5:1
Seventy	Traveling elder (124:139); to preach the gospel to the world and serve as especial witness to the gentiles in all the world (107:25, 34)	70 members, including 7 presidents (107:93)	February 28, 1835	Luke 10:1
High Priest	Standing president (124:134); to preside over stakes and wards and administer in spiritual (107:12) and temporal things (107:71)	No set number, but includes all high priests in the stake	June 3-6, 1831	Hebrews 5:1, 2, 6; 7:11 (notice that both priesthoods are mentioned by name)
Patriarch	Evangelical minister to the gospel through inspired blessings (107:39-40); office "to be handed down from father to son" and belongs to the chosen seed; this order began in the days of Adam (107:40, 41)		December 18, 1833	Acts 21:8
Apostle	Special witness of the name of Christ in all the world (107:23); traveling councilor to ordain and set in order all other offices in the Church (107:58)	12 apostles (107:23, 24, 33)	February 14, 1835	Ephesians 4:11-14 / Matthew 16:19

of the gospel to an individual's life. The office of Patriarch to the Church was passed down from father to son (verse 40), but the patriarchs ordained in the various stakes are not chosen on that basis.

High Priests. Brethren holding this office administer spiritual things and may function in any lesser office. (See verses 10–12.) They are called "standing presidents," the purpose of a high priests quorum being to prepare those who may be called to preside. (See D&C 124:133–35.)

Seventies. Like the Twelve, the seventies are called to be special witnesses; unlike the high priests or elders, the seventies have the major responsibility of being ready to travel when necessary to preach the gospel to the world. Thus, they are called "traveling ministers" or "traveling elders." (Verses 25, 34, 97; D&C 124:138–39).

Elders. The elders are described as "standing ministers" (D&C 124:137), their principal responsibility being to minister in spiritual things at the local level (see D&C 20:38–45; 107:11–12). It should be noted, however, that they may also be asked to travel as missionaries. (See D&C 84:111.)

Bishop. Several revelations in the Doctrine and Covenants throw light on various aspects of the bishop's work. He was to receive consecration and assign stewardships. (See p. 73 for a discussion of the bishop's role in the law of consecration.) Even though he administers temporal things, the bishop is also a spiritual leader with a special endowment of the gift of discernment. (See D&C 46:27.) He is the "common judge in Israel." (See D&C 58:17–18; 107:68–75; also the discussion of section 102 herein for a consideration of the bishop's part in the Church judicial structure.

The firstborn or eldest among the literal descendants of Aaron has a "legal" right to the office of presiding bishop— this because Aaron and his sons were appointed to hold the keys of the lesser priesthood. In the absence of such a person, a high priest may be called to serve as a bishop. (See D&C 68:14–24; 107:15–17, 71–73.) According to section 107, a literal descendant of Aaron could serve without counselors (verse 76) and presumably without having the Melchizedek Priesthood conferred upon him. Even though a bishop might serve as president of the Aaronic Priesthood without counselors or without the high priesthood, he could never act as the head of a ward without counselors to assist him in meeting the many and varied demands of that calling, nor could he correlate ward priesthood activities as presiding high priest without being ordained to the Melchizedek Priesthood.

A bishop actually holds more than one office at a time. For example, if an elder were called and sustained to be a bishop, he would have to be (1) ordained a high priest and (2) ordained a bishop (both of these are permanent priesthood offices); (3) he would then be set apart as "bishop" or as presiding high priest of the specific ward. In this latter ecclesiastical capacity, the bishop corresponds at the local level to the president of the stake and the President of the Church at their respective levels. When he is released he will still be a high priest and bishop, but no longer bishop of the particular ward; if he were subsequently called again to be a bishop, he would not have to be ordained to any new office, but merely set apart in his new calling.

Priest, Teacher, and Deacon. The duties of these three priesthood offices are most completely discussed in section 20:46–59.

Priesthood Quorums

At the core of Church government is the priesthood; surrounding it at the ward, stake, and general levels is the ecclesiastical structure (auxiliaries, committees, programs, etc.). (See Elder Harold B. Lee's discussion on Church organization, *Church News,* August 26, 1961, pp. 8–13.) The priesthood structure is based upon the quorums organized around each of the above priesthood offices (except there are no bishops quorums and no patriarchs quorums). These quorums are designed to help their members function better as priesthood bearers. Section 107 states in general terms that presidencies are to teach quorum members concerning their duties. (See verses 85–89.) These verses also suggest the maximum size of quorums, with the provision that a majority of the total number may constitute a quorum when more are not available. (See verse 28.)

In 1974, however, the First Presidency instructed that an elders quorum should be organized in every ward or independent branch, and that there should be a seventies quorum in every stake even if the formerly required minimum number is not present. (First Presidency circular letter, April 16, 1974; *Church News,* October 19, 1974, p. 10.) Similarly, ward quorums were to be organized for each Aaronic Priesthood office regardless of how few members there might be.

Conclusion (Verses 99-100)

This great revelation on priesthood and Church administration concludes with the most appropriate admonition that each member should learn his respective duties and serve diligently therein and, thus, make his contribution to the overall success of the kingdom of God on earth.

Section 108

Lyman Sherman was first commended for having sought the Lord's counsel through proper channels. (Verse 1.) The counsel in verse 7 is particularly applicable today.

Section 109: Dedicatory Prayer for the Kirtland Temple

Like section 65, this is a prayer given by revelation. It seemed to be directed to the Father but also to Jehovah, the Son whose house was here being dedicated. Both are addressed almost interchangeably. (See, for example, verses 4, 34, and 68.) The Lord inspired the prophet to pray for the fulfillment of earlier instructions and promises concerning the temple. (Compare verses 6-9 with D&C 88:117-120.) This prayer petitions blessings not only for the Church, but also for many other worthy purposes. The Lord was asked to bless the leaders of the Church and their "immediate connections" or relatives. Section 109 set the pattern for subsequent temple dedicatory prayers. They are generally quite lengthy, and their inspired content reflects a review of the greatest concerns to Church leaders at the time.

Kirtland Temple (dedicated 1836) (Photo courtesy Harold B. Lee Library)

The Sacred Hosanna Shout (Verses 79–80). The "Hosanna shout" has been a part of every temple dedication. (This sacred ceremony was also a part of the centennial conference in 1930. See a description in B. H. Roberts, *Comprehensive History of the Church,* vol. 6, p. 540.) The hymn "The Spirit of God like a Fire is Burning" had been written earlier in anticipation of the glorious experiences especially to be associated with the Kirtland Temple. It has been sung at the dedication of all Latter-day Saint temples since that time. It, too—especially in the chorus—reflects this sacred rite.

Section 110: The Restoration of Keys

Statements in the introductory superscription and in this section itself suggest that this revelation came by vision. It is also true, however, that at least Moses, Elias, and Elijah had to appear in person because they conferred keys, which is done by the laying on of hands. (See the discussion on p. 3 concerning the various ways in which revelation comes.) This section consists of a series of manifestations in which glorious beings appear to bring a special message or authority.

Christ (Verses 1–10). The major purpose of the Savior's appearance was to accept the temple which had been dedicated to him just one week earlier. The Lord repeated his earlier promise to manifest himself in his house if no unclean person is permitted to pollute it. (Compare verses 7–8 with D&C 97:15–17.)

Moses (Verse 11). Moses, who gathered the ancient children of Israel and led them to the Promised Land, restored the keys for the latter-day gathering. This gathering is to involve at least five major aspects:

1. The Ten Tribes led by the tribe Ephraim, which were "lost" as a body following the Assyrian conquest in 721 B.C., will return from the north just before the Lord's second coming. (D&C 133:26–27.)

2. The scattered remnants of these same Ten Tribes are being gathered into the Church through missionary work. The first overseas mission was opened in Britain in 1837, the year following the restoration of these keys. At first this gath-

ering was also geographical when it was necessary to build up the strength of the Church in one place; more recently the gathering has been more of a spiritual nature, converts being encouraged to stay in their homelands to build up the Church in preparation for the establishment of stakes. (See D&C 101:20–21.) Even though the seed of Israel was scattered throughout all nations (Amos 9:9), it appears that there has been a heavy concentration of Ephraimites in northern Europe.

3. The remnants of Lehi's people are similarly being gathered by missionary work.

4. The Jewish people are returning to Jerusalem. Even though Orson Hyde dedicated the land of Palestine in 1841, this gathering did not reach major proportions until conditions just after World War II made it possible to establish the state of Israel.

5. Those gentiles (in this case non-Israelites) who become faithful members of Christ's church will be adopted into the covenant people; at the same time, those Israelites who are unfaithful will be cut off. (See 3 Nephi 21:6-11; also Romans 11:13, 17-24.) Thus, those who are faithful will be heirs to the great blessings promised to Abraham's seed. (See D&C 132:31-33.)

Elias (Verse 12). Available sources do not clarify the exact nature of the keys Elias brought. (For a discussion of Elias's identity, see section 27 herein.)

Elijah (Verses 13-16). This appearance fulfilled Malachi's prophecy. (Compare Malachi 4:5-6 with Moroni's clarified version in Section 2. See the discussion under section 3 herein.) The "sealing" key which Elijah restored pertains most especially to the work done in the temples, but not exclusively to work for the dead. Not only do these keys carry the power to bind on earth and have it recognized or bound in heaven (Matthew 16:19), but they also make it possible to secure the necessary "welding links" which bind families together. (See D&C 128:8-18.) The return of the "spirit of Elijah" may be reflected in the sudden increase in genealogical work around the world beginning about the time these keys were restored.

Melchizedek Priesthood pulpits in Kirtland Temple. Here Christ, Moses, Elias, and Elijah appeared. (Photo courtesy Harold B. Lee Library)

(For a full discussion of this most vital subject, see Joseph Fielding Smith, *Doctrines of Salvation*, vol. 2, chap. 6 and 7; also LeGrand Richards, *A Marvelous Work and a Wonder*, chap. 13, "The Mission of Elijah.")

Section 111

The year 1836 was a period of economic distress throughout the United States, and the Saints in Ohio were not immune. Several thousand dollars were still owed for construction of the Kirtland Temple, so Joseph Smith planned a trip to New York to seek financing. When an individual in Kirtland claimed to know the location of some hidden treasure in Salem, Massachusetts, Joseph decided to visit that city as well. At that time there was widespread interest in locating old treasures. Upon reaching Salem, their informant was unable to locate the anticipated treasure. (For a further discussion, see Roberts, *Comprehensive History of the Church*, 1:410-12.) It was in this setting that the Lord reproved the Prophet for his "follies." (D&C 111:1.) The Lord admonished the brethren not to be concerned about the debt. (Verse 5.) Even though he promised that riches would eventually come from the city of Salem (verse 4), he reminded the Prophet that there were more treasures than one for him in the city (verse 10). Joseph Smith was therefore to hire a place where he could stay and preach to the people. He was also encouraged to inquire about the former inhabitants of the area. (Verse 9.)

In light of these instructions, Joseph Smith and his associates spent about a month in Salem preaching the gospel and visiting historic sites. The Prophet also looked into the Smith family genealogy, much of which was found in this area.

Section 112 and Duty of the Twelve

Thomas B. Marsh had become the original president of the Twelve when that group was organized in February 1835. The Twelve were to carry the gospel into the world under the direction of the First Presidency (verses 16-19); the apostles in turn were to have authority to send out others (verse 21; compare D&C 107:34-35). The counsel given to Marsh and the Twelve in verse 10 is relevant to all who strive to serve the Lord.

Apostasy in Kirtland (Verses 23-25). The years 1836 and 1837 were one of the darkest periods in Church history. Many blamed Joseph Smith personally for the failure of the Saints' "Kirtland Safety Society" bank, and a wave of apostasy affected even some in leadership positions. For example, during 1837, Frederick G. Williams apostatized, and therefore Hyrum Smith was called to take his place as second counselor in the First Presidency. This change was reflected in verse 17. Furthermore, on one occasion the Prophet's enemies, with pistols and knives drawn, sought to disrupt a worship service and to take possession of the Kirtland Temple. Section 112 seems to have anticipated these developments. The mission in Great Britain, which opened on the very day this revelation was given, brought converts into the Church who proved to bring new faith and vitality at this critical time.

Section 113

Stem, Rod, and Root of Jesse (Verse 1-6). Like section 77, this revelation includes answers to the Prophet's questions on scripture. Jesse was the father of King David. Even though the "stem of Jesse" is clearly identified as Jesus Christ, it is not known for certain who the "root" and "rod of Jesse" are.

Zion's Strength (Verses 7-8). Reference to latter-day Zion putting on her strength through the priesthood has been fulfilled in part in the Priesthood Correlation Program, which has placed greater responsibilities of priesthood leaders and quorums.

Section 114

David W. Patten, who had stood as the second apostle in seniority, was unable to accompany the quorum on its overseas mission in 1839 as directed in this revelation because he had been killed in the battle of Crooked River on October 25, 1838. Church historians often refer to him as the first martyr of this dispensation.

"Bishopric" (Verse 2). Here this term is used in a broader sense and means "office" or "calling." (Note a similar usage in Acts 1:20 and Psalm 109:8.)

Section 115

Name of the Church (Verse 4). During the first years of its existence, the Church was generally called by its members the Church of Christ or the Church of Jesus Christ, while nonmembers often called it the "Mormonite" Church. In order to avoid the latter name, a conference held May 3, 1834, adopted the official title "The Church of the Latter-day Saints." It is clear from many contemporary sources, however, that the brethren still regarded the Church as being the Church of Jesus Christ. (See B. H. Roberts, *Comprehensive History of the Church,* vol. 1, pp. 392-93.) In 1838, section 115 instructed the members to use the full title of the Church as follows: "The Church of Jesus Christ of Latter-day Saints." The first phrase, "The Church of Jesus Christ," is certainly the key part of the title. (See 1 Corinthians 1:10-13; 3 Nephi 27:8.) The term *Saints* generally refers to those who are sanctified or holy, so the use of this term should be a constant challenge to all Church members. The word *Saints* is also used in a more general sense to refer to members of the Church, all of whom should be seeking sanctification through living the gospel of Jesus Christ. Paul addressed his epistles to the "saints" or church members in various places; he explained that one purpose of the church was the "perfecting of the saints." (See Ephesians 4:11-13.)

Far West: A Gathering Place (Verses 5-19). During the summer of 1837, the citizens of Clay County asked the Mormons to leave in peace, giving as their reasons differences over slavery and Indian policy. As a result, most of the Saints left the area during the fall of that year. About the same time, economic difficulties in Kirtland brought a real crisis—during the opening weeks of 1838, Joseph Smith and those who were loyal to him fled from Ohio to Missouri.

In this revelation the Lord directed his Saints to gather at Far West, Caldwell County, in northern Missouri. This county had been formed expressly for the Mormons, that thereby the Saints' influence could be confined to that one place. The Church was to build a temple according to the pattern the Lord would reveal. They were to begin construction July 4, 1838, and resume work after the winter season, on April 26, just one year after this revelation was given.

In verse 13 the Lord cautioned the First Presidency against going into debt as they had done while building the Kirtland Temple. This counsel may have contributed to the Church's policy of not dedicating buildings until they are fully paid for.

Section 116 and Adam-Ondi-Ahman

This, the shortest section in the Doctrine and Covenants, records the fact that the Lord named a site several miles north of Far West. He named it Adam-Ondi-Ahman because of the great events which have occurred and which will take place there. (See D&C 107:53-57 for an account of the great council Adam held at this place; see also Daniel 7:13-14 and the discussion under section 78 herein for a consideration of

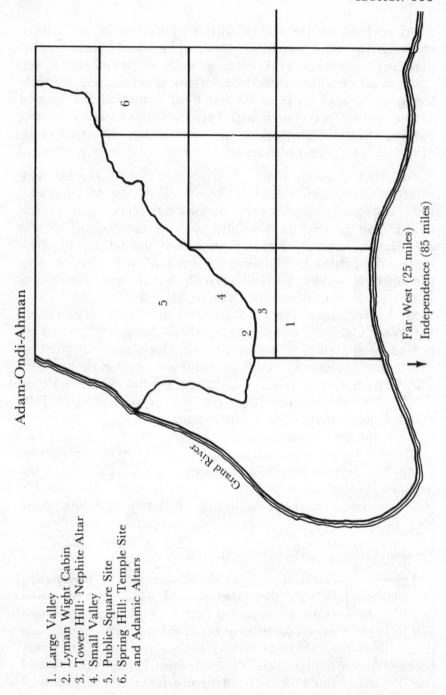

Adam-Ondi-Ahman

Grand River

Far West (25 miles)

Independence (85 miles)

1. Large Valley
2. Lyman Wight Cabin
3. Tower Hill: Nephite Altar
4. Small Valley
5. Public Square Site
6. Spring Hill: Temple Site
   and Adamic Altars

the place and meaning of "Ahman.") Not long before his coming in glory, the Savior will meet Adam and other priesthood leaders from various dispensations. They will turn back to him the keys which they held, thus preparing the way for him to inaugurate his Millennial reign. (For an excellent discussion of this great latter-day conference at Adam-Ondi-Ahman, see Joseph Fielding Smith, *Way to Perfection.*)

Section 117 and the Exodus from Kirtland

Apostasy and bitterness resulted in a mass exodus of faithful Latter-day Saints from Ohio in 1838. On July 6, just two days before this revelation was received, the "Kirtland Camp," consisting of more than five hundred individuals, headed for Missouri. The brethren addressed in section 117 were among those left behind following the general exodus. When Joseph Smith left Kirtland the previous January, he placed Oliver Granger in charge of his business affairs; Granger's integrity was respected even among non-Mormon creditors. (See *HC,* 3:164-65.) As bishop, Newel K. Whitney had similar responsibilities for the Saints' temporal affairs. William Marks did move west as this revelation directed, and later became stake president in Nauvoo.

Nicolaitan Band (Verse 11). John the Revelator declared that the Lord hated the doctrines of the Nicolaitans. (Revelation 2:15.) This ancient group symbolized worldly excess, which probably is the meaning intended in section 117.

Section 118

The wave of apostasy in Ohio even affected the Twelve Apostles; of the four men called in this section to fill the resulting vacancies, two—John Taylor and Wilford Woodruff—later became presidents of the Church, while a third—Willard Richards—became a counselor in the First Presidency.

Earlier revelations had called the Twelve to perform an overseas mission beginning during the spring of 1839 (D&C 114:1), and also directed that construction on the Far West Temple be renewed on April 26 of that year (D&C 115:8-11). Section 118 now instructed the Twelve to leave for their mission from Far West on the above date. (Verses 5-6.) During the winter of 1838-39, however, the Latter-day Saints fled from Missouri under the governor's threat of extermination if they remained in the state. Non-Mormons openly boasted that these circumstances would prevent the Twelve from keeping the above commandment and, thus, prove Joseph Smith to be a false prophet. But, the apostles returned to Far West at great personal risk, and early in the morning of April 26, 1839, they laid the cornerstone of the temple and then prepared to depart for their missions. It was on this occasion that Wilford Woodruff was ordained an apostle.

Section 119 and the Law of Tithing

Those to whom this revelation was originally given had been living the law of consecration. For them, the "beginning of the tithing" consisted of giving their surpluses to the bishop. (See verses 1 and 3.) More recently, the law of tithing has consisted of giving one-tenth of one's "interest" annually or as earned. The First Presidency has explained that *interest* "is understood to mean *income*." (First Presidency circular letter, March 19, 1970; italics added.) Elder Howard W. Hunter added: "Interest means profit, compensation, increase. It is the wage of one employed, the profit from the operation of a business, the increase of one who grows or produces, or the income of a person from any other source." (*CR*, April 1964, pp. 33-36.)

The Lord has promised great blessings to those who keep this law. (See Malachi 3:8-10; D&C 64:23.) Latter-day prophets have taught that those who pay an honest tithing will always prosper. This does not necessarily mean immediate financial return, but it does mean that the Lord will bless the faithful with those things most important to their overall well-being. Because tithing is the Lord's law of revenue, those who pay are helping to build his kingdom and thereby share more fully in the blessings which his Church can bring. (See verse 2 and Chart 17.) Despite the promised blessings, it is hoped that one pays tithing primarily because he loves the Lord. (See John 14:15. For statements made by presidents of the Church about tithing, see Daniel H. Ludlow, *Latter-day Prophets Speak,* pp. 323-34.)

Chart 17

The Lord's Law of Revenue

Percentage of Tithing and Other General
Church Funds Spent for Various Purposes*

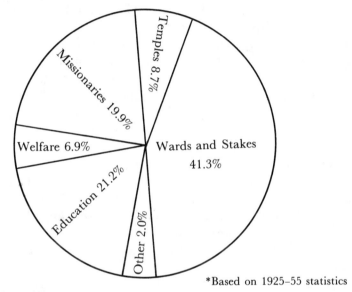

Temples 8.7%

Missionaries 19.9%

Welfare 6.9%

Education 21.2%

Other 2.0%

Wards and Stakes
41.3%

*Based on 1925–55 statistics

Section 120: The Disposition of Tithes

According to these instructions, the Committee on the Disposition of Tithes shall consist of the First Presidency, the High Council (meaning the presiding traveling high council composed of the Twelve Apostles), and the Presiding Bishopric. These men are to handle tithing funds as they are inspired by the Lord. Currently a subcommittee, the Expenditures Committee, consisting of the First Presidency, three of the Twelve Apostles, and the Presiding Bishopric, makes specific decisions within general guidelines set forth by the Committee on the Disposition of Tithes. (See statement by President J. Reuben Clark, Jr., *CR*, April 1948, pp. 116–17.)

Sections 121–23: At Liberty Jail

For several years Latter-day Saint settlement in Missouri had met intense opposition. During the fall of 1838 difficulties flared anew. (See chronology below.) A series of attacks on outlying Mormon settlements led on October 25 to a clash between the Saints and their enemies on the banks of Crooked River; several lost their lives, including Apostle David W. Patten. Two days later Governor Boggs described the Saints as being in "open and avowed defiance of the laws" and as "having made war upon the people of the state," so he ordered that "the Mormons must be treated as enemies and must be exterminated or driven from the state." With this encouragement, a mob attacked Haun's Mill on October 30 and killed seventeen Saints. The following day Far West itself surrendered, and Joseph Smith and other Church leaders were taken as prisoners. That winter some 12,000 to 15,000 Saints were forced to flee from Missouri.

Meanwhile, the prisoners were "exhibited" in Independence, and were then taken to Richmond to await trial. Elder Parley P. Pratt described how one night the guards boasted obscenely of evils committed against the Latter-day Saints. Although chained, Joseph Smith suddenly arose and thundered:

SILENCE, *ye fiends of the infernal pit. In the name of Jesus Christ I rebuke you, and command you to be still; I will not live another minute and hear such language. Cease such talk, or you or I die* THIS INSTANT!

The guards immediately ceased their boastings and begged the Prophet's pardon. Elder Pratt, in recalling his experiences with the leaders of the world, concluded, "Dignity and majesty have I seen but *once,* as it stood in chains, at midnight, in a dungeon in an obscure vilage in Missouri." (*Autobiography of Parley P. Pratt,* p. 211.) It may be to this incident that Doctrine and Covenants 122:4 refers.

Following a preliminary hearing in November of 1838, the prisoners were transferred to the jail in Liberty, Missouri, to await a trial which never came. Throughout the winter the brethren suffered from inadequate ventilation, heating, and

Liberty Jail (Photo courtesy Harold B. Lee Library)

sanitation; their food was grossly inferior, and they had nothing but the rough stone floor for a bed. It was in the circumstances that the revelations contained in sections 121, 122, and 123 were received. Shortly after this time, Missouri state officials became increasingly embarrassed over the Church leaders' being held in jail on ill-founded charges, so allowed them to "escape." The Prophet and his associates made their way to Illinois where they rejoined the Saints.

Culmination of Missouri Persecutions

1838. Aug. 6	Mob oppose Saints voting at Gallatin, Missouri.	
Oct. 11	Saints driven from DeWitt, and later from other settlements.	
Oct. 25	Apostle David W. Patten killed during clash with mob at Crooked River.	
Oct. 27	Governor orders that Mormons be exterminated or driven from Missouri.	
Oct. 30	Seventeen Saints massacred at Haun's Mill.	
Oct. 31	Joseph Smith and others taken prisoner by mob militia.	
Nov. 1	Far West surrendered	
Nov. 9	Prisoners arrive in Richmond, Missouri.	
Nov. 28	Joseph Smith and others transferred to jail in Liberty, Missouri.	
1839 March	Sections 121-123 written from Liberty Jail	
April 16	Joseph Smith and fellow prisoners "escape."	

The Prophet's prayer (D&C 121:1-6) reflects the months of suffering which he and his associates had endured in the Liberty Jail. It should be realized that Joseph Smith had actually experienced all the trials mentioned in the subsequent revelation. (See D&C 122:5-7.) The Lord's answers to the Prophet's pleas (D&C 121:7-25 and section 122) compared these afflictions to those suffered by Job and by the Lord himself and, thus, set them in their proper perspective. The Prophet was told that these things were to give him experience "and shall be for thy good." (D&C 122:7.)

As the Prophet reflected on these things (D&C 121:26-46), he could see that the Saints had truly been blessed with unprecedented revelations and manifestations through the Holy Ghost. In verse 33 he expressed the idea that it would be as impossible for men to prevent the Lord from blessing his people as it would be for them to stop the Missouri River or divert it from its course.   Verses 34-40 warn that sin and pride undermine priesthood power; verses 41-44 set forth the spirit in which priesthood authority must be exercised. Verses 45-46 promise that the virtuous will not be ashamed of their lives, but that their "confidence [shall] wax strong in the presence of God," and that the Holy Ghost shall be their constant companion. The profound ideas and beauty of expression here (verses 34-46) rank among the greatest passages in the world's literature.

Amen to the Priesthood (D&C 121:37). If a man becomes unrighteous, his priesthood which he does not magnify will become a source of personal condemnation rather than a blessing for him. His ability to bless others through his priesthood will be impaired, and he should not be called to represent the Lord or the Church in performing sacred ordinances. If one's unworthiness is not known and those in authority call him to perform an ordinance, the ordinance is valid because the person performs it not so much by his own authority but, rather, acts as a duly appointed agent for the Church. The efficacy of ordinances depends more on the worthiness of those receiving than upon the worthiness of those performing them.

Section 124 and the Establishment of Nauvoo

About two years had passed since the Latter-day Saints had fled from Missouri. In addition to the major ideas about building the new city of Nauvoo, this revelation contains many items of instruction to many specific individuals. Of particular interest is the Lord's request in verses 103–105 that Sidney Rigdon remain with the Saints and locate his family near Joseph Smith's residence so that he might be of greater assistance to the Prophet. It will be remembered that at the time of the martyrdom (three and a half years later), Rigdon had moved from Nauvoo to Pittsburgh in opposition to the above instructions. Apparently there were some who wondered if the Church should at that time return to Kirtland, but in verse 83 the Lord definitely answered that question in the negative.

Two Buildings for Nauvoo

The Nauvoo Temple (Verses 25–55). The Lord explained that those who do all that is possible to keep his commandments but are thwarted by the opposition of others will not be held accountable, but the penalties of the broken law will come upon those enemies who prevented it from being kept. In this spirit, the Lord would not hold the Saints responsible for failing to build his temple in Missouri, but because of their good faith he would give them another opportunity by having them build a temple in Nauvoo. (See verses 49–55.)

One of the major purposes of building this temple was to provide a place where the Lord could come and restore "the fulness of the priesthood." (Verses 27–28.) Verse 39 lists some of the specific functions of the temple, including baptism for the dead, endowments, washings and anointings, memorials of certain Levitical offerings (or record of such sacrifices; see the discussion of "Levites" offering under section 13 herein), and oracles in holy places by which revelation comes. All these things are for the building up of Zion and her "municipalities" or units, such as stakes, etc.

The Lord particularly reminded the Church that there was no font where baptism for the dead could be performed—

Nauvoo Temple (Photo courtesy Harold B. Lee Library)

Joseph Smith having taught this doctrine as early as 1840. These ordinances were performed in the Mississippi River until the temple font was completed. The Nauvoo Temple, when built, was essentially the same in design as the Kirtland Temple, with the major addition of a baptismal font in the basement story. This matter was of sufficient importance that the Lord warned his Church that it would be rejected if these ordinances were not being performed in his house by the end of a given period of time. (See verses 31–33.) Some apostate groups have asserted that the Lord's conditions were not met and, as a result, the Church was rejected. It is interesting to note, however, that none of these splinter groups perform the work for the dead as done by the Church they criticize.

Perhaps the "fulness of the priesthood" was to be restored most completely through the instructions and ordinances belonging to the temple endowment. The Savior promised to reveal to Joseph Smith "things which have been kept hid from before the foundation of the world, things that pertain to the dispensation of the fulness of times. And I will show unto my servant Joseph all things pertaining to this house, and the priesthood thereof." (Verses 41–42.) In preparation for giving the endowment in the temple when completed, the Prophet gave this ordinance to a select group in his office on May 4, 1842.

The Nauvoo Temple was not yet completed when Joseph Smith was martyred in 1844. As persecution mounted and the Saints prepared for their westward exodus, they felt a compelling need to finish the temple and to receive the sacred blessings available in the House of the Lord. The structure was sufficiently completed by December, 1845, that the endowment could be given there. The temple was not formally dedicated until May 1, 1846, several weeks after the majority of the Saints had been forced to flee from their "City Beautiful." The temple was subsequently burned by a mob, and its remaining stone walls were toppled by a tornado several years later.

The Nauvoo House (Verses 22–24, 56–122). This building was to fill the need in Nauvoo for a hotel or boarding house. It was not merely to be a commercial venture but was to provide the opportunity to share the gospel with travelers who might wish to stop there. (See verses 23 and 60.) Therefore, investors had to meet not only the usual economic criteria but also were to have a testimony of the gospel. (See verse 119.) The brethren were to form a "quorum" (not a priesthood quorum) or building committee to supervise the project. The provision that Joseph Smith's heirs were to have their place in the house forever (verses 56–59) had nothing to do with the idea of lineal succession in the presidency but merely conformed to the policy which applied to all others who invested in this venture. (See verse 69.) Nevertheless, the promise made in verses 57–58 should be taken as a personal challenge by anyone who may be among Joseph Smith's descendants.

The Nauvoo House was not finished before the Saints were forced to flee from Illinois. Many years later, the partially completed building was finished on a smaller scale than originally planned, and presently is operated by the Reorganized Church as a hostel.

Priesthood Instruction

First Presidency Reorganized (Verses 91–96). These verses directed a reorganization within the First Presidency. William Law was named second counselor to take the place of Hyrum Smith, who was being released to accept two other positions (see biographical sketch of Hyrum Smith, section 11 herein.) Hyrum, being the eldest son of Joseph Smith, Sr., who had died a few months earlier, was called to succeed his father as Patriarch to the Church, according to the pattern set in Doctrine and Covenants 107:40. Hyrum was also to occupy the office of Assistant President held by Oliver Cowdery before his apostasy. It will be recalled that Oliver had been sustained as the "second elder" next to Joseph Smith in authority when the Church was organized in 1830. On December 5, 1834, following the organization of the First Presidency, Joseph Smith set him apart as Assistant President. (See *HC,* 2:176.) Cowdery was not only to assist the Prophet in administering to the Church, but he was to stand with him as the second witness of the Restoration, he having been with Joseph Smith when the keys to the priesthood were restored. Section 124, verses 94–96, now called Hyrum to assume this responsibility—the Lord promising to show him the things of which he was to bear record. Thus, the two brothers who gave their lives at the Carthage Jail stood as the two presidents and witnesses to seal their testimonies with their blood. (For a discussion of the Assistant President, see Joseph Fielding Smith, *Doctrines of Salvation,* vol. 1, pp. 211–22.)

Church Organization Outlined (Verses 123-145). In the concluding verses of section 124, the Lord listed the various offices which were to be filled and for which room was to be provided in the temple. These leaders were to hold keys by which they might give direction to those bearing the priesthood. (See "Priesthood Offices and Quorums" under section 107 herein for a consideration of the nature and duties of these callings.)

Section 125

Organization of the Zarahemla or Iowa Stake reflected Church settlement across the Mississippi River from Nauvoo.

Section 126

Brigham Young had stood third in seniority among the original apostles. When Thomas B. Marsh apostatized and David W. Patten was killed, Elder Young became the new President of the Twelve. Just before the time of this revelation, he had completed a successful mission in Britain.

Sections 127–28: Epistles on Baptism for the Dead

During May 1842, Governor Lilburn Boggs of Missouri, who issued the extermination order against the Mormons, was shot and wounded. The Latter-day Saints were immediately suspected, and Joseph Smith was accused of being an accessory to the crime. During August, the Illinois governor finally yielded to Missouri's demands and had the Prophet arrested, but Joseph was soon released. Some Missourians then threatened to cross the river into Illinois and seize Joseph Smith by force. At this point, the Prophet went into hiding for the safety of both the Church and himself. It was in this setting that he wrote the two letters dated September first and sixth, which are now sections 127 and 128, respectively, in the Doctrine and Covenants.

The Need for a Recorder. In his first letter (D&C 127:5-9), Joseph Smith emphasized the importance of having a recorder present when baptisms for the dead were performed, not only to make a record but also to be a witness that the ordinance was done properly. The Prophet returned to this same theme in his second epistle and linked the idea of making a record of valid ordinances to the power of binding and sealing on earth and having these acts recognized in heaven. (See D&C 128:3-10.)

General and Ward Recorders (D&C 128:3-4). The reference in verse 3 is the first mention of the "ward" in the Doctrine and Covenants. This is a common political subdivision. It appears that Nauvoo was divided into wards for both political and ecclesiastical purposes. Even though there had been bishops in the Church since 1831, they were first associated with ward units in Nauvoo. The appointment of a general Church recorder (verse 4) marked the beginning of the Church Historian and Recorder as a formal office. Willard Richards was the first to hold this position, although Oliver Cowdery and John Whitmer had been called earlier to keep histories. (See discussion of section 47 herein.)

Baptism for the Dead (Verses 12-13). Baptism is a symbol of death, burial, and resurrection. Therefore, immersion is the proper mode, and the baptismal font is generally located on a lower level in similitude of the grave. (See D&C 128:12-13).

Importance of Work for the Dead. (Verses 15-18). In stressing the importance of vicarious work for the dead, Joseph Smith amplified the meaning of several biblical passages. For example, Paul taught that the dead cannot be made perfect without us (Hebrews 11:40); Joseph Smith added the thought that we without them cannot be made perfect (see D&C 128:15). Furthermore, commenting on Malachi's prophecy of Elijah's coming, Joseph Smith stressed the need of a "welding link" between generations and dispensations. (Verses 17–18.) He therefore, called on the Saints to be prepared to present in the temple an offering of an acceptable record of their dead. (See D&C 128:24.) (For other thoughts on the work for the dead, see the discussion of Elijah's mission under sections 2 and 110 herein.)

Restoration of the Gospel (Verses 19–21). As the Prophet reviewed some of the glorious events which have been part of the Restoration, he called on the people to rejoice. In these verses, he gave information about certain events which is not found anywhere else. The exact area where the Melchizedek Priesthood was restored is specified here. The voice of God heard in the Whitmers' chamber was part of the circumstances leading to the reception of section 18. There is no other information about appearances of Michael (Adam). Perhaps the coming of Gabriel refers to the appearance of Elias in the Kirtland Temple. (See the discussion about the identity of Elias under section 27 herein.) The exact identity of Raphael is unknown.

On to the Victory! (Verses 22–23). In our own day Church leaders have often quoted and renewed the challenge given by Joseph Smith in the first part of verse 22.

Section 129: Angels and Spirits

To better identify the classes of supernatural messengers, one may list the various stages in the life of a spirit as follows: unembodied (in the preearthly existence), embodied (during mortality, including translated beings), disembodied (following death), and reembodied (resurrected).

In elaborating on the teachings in this revelation, Joseph Smith pointed out that there are two classes of beings in heaven:

1. "Angels," which are heavenly beings possessing tangible bodies either translated or resurrected. (Note that this is a

more precise usage of the term *angel,* which is often used to refer to all heavenly messengers in general.)

2. "Ministering spirits," which may be either unembodied or disembodied. (See *HC,* 4:425.) Because the sons of perdition will not be resurrected until after the Millennium, all messengers from Satan's kingdom must be spirits. (See Chart 18 below, which lists the various kinds of beings.)

Chart 18

Types of Messengers

	Spirit Only	With Body
Heaven	Ministering spirits of just men made perfect (unembodied or disembodied)	Angels Translated (embodied) and Resurrected (reembodied)
Hades	Satan and his emissaries (unembodied or disembodied)	

Section 130

While on a short trip to Ramus, Illinois, with the Prophet, Elder Orson Hyde delivered a sermon on 1 John 3:2, suggesting that the Savior will come as a warrior and that we would be like him, having some of that same spirit. Afterward, the Prophet offered some corrections about the Second Coming, and these and other items are included in section 130. (See *HC,* 5:323.)

The Second Coming

Personal Appearance (Verses 1-3). These verses emphasize the personal character of the Christ at the Second Coming and suggest that we will be like the Savior because he is a person. Unlike us, however, he is a resurrected, glorified, celestial being. In verse 22 the Prophet gave what is perhaps the clearest single statement about the bodily nature of each member of the Godhead. These teachings agree with numerous biblical passages in which persons who have seen God describe him in corporeal terms. (See, for example, Genesis 1:27; Exodus 24:9–11; 33:11, 21–23; Acts 7:55–56; Hebrews 1:1–3.)

When Will He Come? (Verses 4–11, 14–17). The Prophet taught that God, like us, reckons time according to the planet on which he resides. (Compare Abraham 3:3–4.) In verses 6–11 the Lord deviated from the theme of the Second Coming to comment on the nature of the world on which God resides and the nature of our earth when it becomes celestialized. The earth will be like a giant Urim and Thummim by which its inhabitants can behold inferior kingdoms; in addition, each person will have his personal Urim and Thummim by which he can see greater kingdoms—other celestial worlds in a more advanced state of progression. (See "History of the Earth," under section 77 herein.)

In verses 14–17 the Lord answered a question which the Prophet had apparently persisted in asking. Some critics have asserted that in these verses Joseph Smith taught that the Second Coming would occur in 1890 (he having been born in 1805) and that the failure of fulfillment proved him a false prophet. Note, to the contrary, that the Prophet himself questioned that this referred to the beginning of the Millennium. The fact is that he did not live to be eighty-five years old, so the required conditions were not met. Some have suggested that if the Prophet had lived that long, he might have been able to prepare the people to receive the Lord; but this is mere conjecture.

Other Items of Instruction

Civil War Prophecy (Verses 12–13). Joseph Smith referred to this prophecy which had been given in 1832. (See the discussion of section 87 herein.)

Intelligence (Verses 18–19). The intelligence and knowledge mentioned in these verses may include worldly learning, but undoubtedly go far beyond. Note that these are to be acquired through diligence but also through obedience. (See the discussion of "Intelligence" under section 93 herein.)

Law and Obedience (Verses 20–21). In order for man to have true free agency—

1. there must be a law, obedience or disobedience to which brings consequences,

2. man must have a knowledge of these alternatives and their consequences, and

3. he must have the freedom to choose.

Here the Prophet teaches the direct relationship between obedience to law and blessings. (See the discussion under section 19 herein of God's justice as it is related to the atonement of Jesus Christ.)

Section 131

Divisions within the Celestial Kingdom (Verses 1–4). This is the clearest scriptural statement concerning the internal structure of the celestial kingdom. Only those who are in the highest of the three divisions are "exalted." (See the discussion of the celestial kingdom under section 76, and the discussion of celestial marriage under section 132 herein.)

Man Cannot Be Saved in Ignorance (Verses 5–6). Some have supposed that these verses teach that secular knowledge is essential to salvation. It is true that in order to become as God one must have all knowledge; but when taken together, these verses suggest that the knowledge necessary for entrance into the celestial kingdom is a spiritual knowledge. At some point during progression, all who will eventually be exalted must reach the point at which they have so demonstrated their worthiness that the Lord is able through the Spirit to assure them that they will receive the highest glory in the celestial kingdom. It is possible through living the gospel to receive this "more sure word of prophecy" and make one's "calling and election sure" while still in mortality. This is the challenge to all Latter-day Saints. (See "The Holy Spirit of Promise," pp. 110, 125 herein. Sidney B. Sperry's treatment of sections 131 and 132 also gives valuable insights—see *Doctrine and Covenants Compendium,* pp. 700–738.)

Spirit Is Matter (Verses 7–8). Most traditional theologies advance a philosophy of dualism by teaching that spirit and matter are opposites. These verses, however, suggest a philosophy of monism—that spirit and matter are of similar substance but are of a different order or degree of refinement. A resurrected body, for example, is quickened by the spirit rather than by blood so is more refined than a mortal body; yet such a body is still tangible, being of coarser nature than a spirit. This difference in perfection may account for the contrast drawn in the scriptures between the willing spirit and the relatively weaker or more evil flesh. (See, for example, Matthew 26:41; 2 Ne. 2:27-29.)

Section 132 and Celestial Marriage

The teachings in this revelation were received as early as the fall of 1831, when Joseph Smith was preparing his inspired revision of the Bible. He had asked if the ancient patriarchs committed adultery by having more than one wife (see verses 1 and 41). The superscription's statement that this revelation was "recorded" rather than "given" on July 12, 1843, suggests that it was received at some earlier time. Over the years, most nonmembers have thought that the Latter-day Saint doctrine of celestial marriage meant *plural* marriage. This revelation, however, teaches that celestial marriage means *eternal* marriage.

Celestial or Eternal Marriage

Latter-day Saints believe that in order for one to be exalted and obtain godhood in the celestial kingdom, one must abide all aspects of the "new and everlasting covenant"—the gospel (D&C 66:2), including the covenant of eternal marriage. (See D&C 131:1-4 and the discussion of the celestial kingdom under section 76 herein; see also "Marriage Is Ordained of God," under section 49 herein.) In order for a marriage to be a valid celestial marriage, it must meet at least two requirements:

1. It must include a covenant not only for time but also for eternity.

2. It must be performed by the authority of the priesthood.

A third requirement must also be met to make the marriage effective: it must be sealed by the Holy Spirit of Promise; or in other words, those involved must be worthy to receive the promised blessings. (See verses 7–18).

Promised Blessings (Verses 19–24). Those who are faithful to the celestial marriage covenant are promised the greatest of all blessings—they may become gods and share in the fullness of our Father's glory. They are assured that they will come forth in the first resurrection, having necessary knowledge so that they will be able to pass by the angels set to guard the way to exaltation. They will receive the blessing of "eternal increase," "continuation of the seed," or "eternal lives," meaning that they alone will have the power of procreation by which they may bring forth spirit offspring to people the other worlds they create.

On the other hand, those who do not abide this covenant cannot be gods, but rather are angels or "ministering servants" to those who are exalted; they must remain "separately and singly" and "cannot have an increase." (D&C 131:4; 132:16–17.)

These blessings are promised on the condition that the person does not commit the unpardonable sin. President Joseph Fielding Smith pointed out that verse 26 does not promise exaltation unconditionally. He suggests that setting this verse in the context of other scriptural teachings shows that these blessings may come only on condition of repentance. (See Joseph Fielding Smith, *Doctrines of Salvation,* vol. 2, pp. 94–99.)

The Three Most Serious Sins. Alma spoke of sins in an order of seriousness (see Alma 39:5–6):

1. Denying the witness of the Holy Ghost after having received it and permanently turning away from and fighting against the Lord is an unpardonable sin. (See the discussion of pardon and forgiveness, p. 45.) Thus, those who can commit this sin must first have experienced God's power and then denied it. (See Matthew 12:31–32; Hebrews 6:4–6; 2 Peter 2:21–22; 1 John 5:16; D&C 76:32, 35.) In a sense, such offenders shed "innocent blood" in that they would assent to the Lord's death. (See D&C 132:27.) Those who commit this sin will become sons of perdition.

2. Murder. (See D&C 42:18.) Although most murderers may attain the telestial kingdom, such an offense is unpardonable for those who know the gospel through the Spirit and have entered into sacred covenants with the Lord.

3. Adultery. (See D&C 42:24-25, 76-77.) These last two sins are *pardonable, but not forgivable* under many circumstances, because it is either impossible or very difficult to repent and make restitution.

Plural Marriage

Polygamy vs. Adultery. If adultery be defined as illicit relationships (verses 41-43), then plural marriages cannot be adultery because the husband receives his wives by recognized authority (see verses 61-62). It was in this light that the Lord justified the ancient patriarchs in their plural marriage relationships. For example, the Lord said that he had given to David and Solomon their many wives and concubines and that they sinned only when they took that which was not given them by the Lord. (See verse 38.)

Some have questioned this last passage about David and Solomon in the light of Book of Mormon teachings. According to Jacob, chapter 2, the Nephites were excusing themselves in immorality because they did not fully understand the scriptural accounts of David's and Solomon's having many wives and concubines—considered an abomination before the Lord. (See Jacob 2:23-24; also 1 Kings 11:3.) These two verses should be read as conveying one thought, because both composed a single sentence in the earliest edition of the Book of Mormon, before it was divided into verses. In this light, the abomination could refer either to the people's committing whoredoms or to David's and Solomon's many wives and concubines. D&C 132:38 eliminates the latter alternative, and Jacob specifically identifies whoredoms as the abomination. (See Jacob 2:28.) There can be no doubt but that the Nephites were commanded to live in monogamy (verse 27); nevertheless, the Lord suggested the possibility that this commandment might be changed at some future time (see Jacob 2:30).

Purposes of Polygamy The faithful Latter-day Saints who entered this "difficult" marriage relationship did so because of their faith that it was a divinely appointed institution. The Lord revealed it perhaps for many of the same reasons which led him to give the law of consecration—it was an essential part of the restoration of all things (verse 45) and a preparation for possible things to come. The Lord further explained that he instituted plural marriage so that his people could "multiply and replenish the earth . . . that they may bear the souls of men." (Verse 63). (For a consideration of the subsequent history of plural marriage in the Church, see the discussion of the Official Declaration, pp. 207–10.)

Section 133: The Appendix

Because this section is designated "The Appendix," it stands at the end of the revelations given through Joseph Smith—sections 134, 135, and 136 being of a different order. This revelation was given a day or so after section 67 was received at the conference considering publication of the first compilation of revelations. Another revelation given at about the same time, known as "the Lord's Preface," now stands as section 1. Notice that many of the ideas in the "Preface" are paralleled in section 133. (See the discussion of section 1 herein.)

The Command to Gather (Verses 1–15). This revelation was given to answer the elders' questions concerning what they should preach. Verses 7–9 directed that the missionaries' message should be a call for gathering. For several decades the Perpetual Emigrating Fund and other Church programs assisted converts in "gathering to Zion" or, in other words, actually leaving home to join the main body of saints in America. Today the missionaries' message is still "gather," but more in the sense suggested in verse 14; this is a spiritual gathering out of the wicked world into the community of Saints who are building strong branches of the Church in their respective homelands.

Events Surrounding Christ's Second Coming

To stress the urgency of the above message, the Lord reviewed some of the great events to be associated with his second advent. (See the discussion of the signs of the times under section 45 herein.)

Geographical Changes (Verses 22-29). Massive changes in climate and topography will be part of the earth's receiving its paradisiacal glory as the Millennium begins. (See the discussion of the earth's history under section 77 herein.) Verses 23 and 24 indicate that these changes will even include the relocation of continents. Recently discovered evidence has led scientists to consider more seriously the idea that our separate continents were originally one landmass. In the midst of these great changes, the lost ten tribes of Israel will return. (Verses 26-28.) The circumstances of their return will be considered even more miraculous than Moses' parting of the Red Sea. (See Isaiah 35:8-10; Jeremiah 16:14-15; see also the discussion of the Ten Tribes under section 110 herein.)

The Lord's Appearance (Verses 38-51). The Lord's coming will be a time of rejoicing for the righteous, but it will be a time of judgment for the wicked. Verse 41 identifies the presence of the Lord's glory as the source of the fire which will consume the wicked. Even the red color of his clothing will be symbolic of the judgments upon the wicked and of his atoning blood. (Compare verses 46-48 with Isaiah 63:2-3.)

Resurrected with Christ (Verses 54-55). This list of those "who were with Christ in his resurrection" includes several who originally were translated (see the discussion of translated beings under section 7 herein): Enoch and his city, Moses, and Noah (see the discussion of Elias being Noah under section 27 herein). These individuals could not have been resurrected earlier because Christ was to be the "first fruits" of the resurrection.

Moses and Elias (or Elijah) needed to retain their mortal bodies (through being translated) so that they could bestow keys at the Mount of Transfiguration by the laying on of hands prior to the time of the Lord's resurrection.

"These Commandments" (Verses 60-64). The "commandments" were the Lord's revelations about to be published in the

Book of Commandments, of which section 133 was to be the "Appendix." Those who receive these things were and are promised eternal life, while those who reject them will suffer the judgments outlined in this and preceding revelations. In his "Preface," revealed a day or so earlier, the Lord had described this book as a "voice of warning . . . unto all people." (D&C 1:4.) The degree to which we heed this warning will determine our eternal destiny.

Section 134: Declaration on Governments and Laws

This statement, written by Oliver Cowdery on behalf of the First Presidency, was adopted at the same conference which approved the 1835 edition of the Doctrine and Covenants for publication. In the light of recent persecution and the apparent ineffectiveness of civil government in protecting the Saints, the brethren felt the need for clarifying the Church's stand.

Responsibility to Obey the Law. The twelfth Article of Faith states: "We believe in being subject to kings, presidents, rulers, and magistrates, in obeying, honoring, and sustaining the law." This blanket statement is qualified somewhat in two Doctrine and Covenants passages. Section 134, verse 5, states that the Saints are "bound to sustain and uphold" their "respective governments . . . while protected in their inherent and inalienable rights by the laws of such governments." Section 98, verse 5, requires not only that the law support basic rights and privileges but that it must also be Constitutional. These conditions make the Saints' obligation to obey and sustain the law of the land more reasonable.

Church and State. Both civil governments and religion were instituted by God for the good of mankind. (See verses 1 and 4.) Yet, according to verse 9, one should not unduly dominate the other. Still there is not total separation, because religion may appeal to the state for protection (verse 11) and must also seek and uphold wise and good men in government (see D&C 98:10). On the other hand, the state may not interfere with religious beliefs unless they prompt practices which infringe on the rights of others or result in crime. (See verse 4.)

The United States Constitution includes three provisions regarding religion:

1. Congress (the national government) cannot establish an official state church.

2. Congress cannot infringe upon freedom of worship.

3. There can be no religious qualifications or test for holding public office.

Section 135: An Appraisal of Joseph Smith

John Taylor was well qualified to write this statement. Not only was he an eyewitness to the martyrdom, but his position as one of the Twelve Apostles enabled him to assess the spiritual significance of the Prophet's contributions. (Consider, for example, the lofty claim set forth in verse 3.) With their deaths, Joseph and Hyrum Smith sealed their testimonies with their blood. (See Hebrews 9:16–17. For a discussion of Hyrum's unique standing at this time, see "Priesthood Instructions," under section 124 herein.)

Carthage Jail (Photo courtesy Harold B. Lee Library)

Brigham Young (Photo courtesy Harold B. Lee Library)

Section 136 and the Pioneers

This revelation is of interest because it was given to Brigham Young, the second great prophet and president of the Church. Many of these inspiring exhortations and practical instructions can help Latter-day Saints today as much as they helped those who had been driven from their homes in Illinois and who were about to cross the Great Plains to a new home in the Rocky Mountains.

Section 137: Joseph Smith's Vision of the Celestial Kingdom

This revelation was added to the standard works in 1976. (See the discussion under section 138 herein.) It was received at a special meeting of Church leaders in the nearly completed Kirtland Temple on Thursday, January 21, 1836. That evening, after the School of the Prophets had been dismissed, these leaders received their washings and anointings. Joseph Smith then recorded his vision of the celestial kingdom (section 137) and of the labors of the Twelve in far-off lands. Of this occasion, the Prophet wrote: "Many of my brethren who received the ordinance [of washing and anointing] with me saw glorious visions also. Angels ministered unto them as well as to myself, and the power of the Highest rested upon us, the house was filled with the glory of God, and we shouted Hosanna to God and the Lamb. . . . Some of them saw the face of the Savior [and] we all communed with the heavenly host." (*HC* 2:379-82.)

Glory of the Celestial Kingdom (Verses 1-4). Human language is inadequate to describe fully the "transcendent beauty" of the celestial kingdom, yet specific qualities are suggested by the symbols the Lord has employed: References to the "blazing" throne of God and to "circling flames of fire" are consistent with the physical brilliance characteristic of celestial beings. (See for example JS-H 1:16-17 and 30-32.) Describing the celestialized earth as "a sea of glass" (D&C 77:1) emphasizes its purity, while likening it to a "great Urim and Thummim" (D&C 130:8) focuses on the knowledge which will be available to its exalted inhabitants. Since earthly roads are paved with coarse materials, depicting heavenly streets as having the appearance of gold (D&C 137:4) serves to heighten our sense of their exquisite beauty.

Salvation for the Dead (Verses 5-9). When Joseph Smith saw his brother Alvin in the celestial kingdom (D&C 137:5), this was a vision of the future; his father and mother, whom he also saw in that kingdom, were still alive. Vicarious baptisms, inaugurated just four years after this vision was received, would extend the opportunity of salvation to those who died without hearing the gospel. The Lord's affirmation in verses 7-9 clarifies that even those who receive the gospel in the spirit world may still qualify for celestial glory. (See the discussion under D&C 76:73 herein.)

Status of Little Children (Verse 10). They will have the same opportunity to earn their exaltation as though they had lived to maturity. President Joseph F. Smith explained: "They will not be deprived of the blessings that belong to them . . . and in the wisdom and mercy and economy of God our Heavenly Father, all that could have been obtained and enjoyed by them if they had been permitted to live in the flesh will be provided for them hereafter." (*Gospel Doctrine,* p. 453.) Elder Joseph Fielding Smith added: "Every privilege to obtain the exaltation given to mortals will be given to those who die in infancy." (*Answers to Gospel Questions,* 1:59.)

Section 138: Vision of the Redemption of the Dead

This revelation is the only numbered section in the Doctrine and Covenants which was received in the twentieth century or in Utah, where the headquarters of the Church are now located. Sections 137 and 138 were added to the standard works in 1976, at first being assigned to the Pearl of Great Price. Five years later they were transferred to their present position as part of the new 1981 edition of the Doctrine and Covenants. Thus they followed the pattern of section 87, which also had been a part of the Pearl of Great Price before it was moved to the Doctrine and Covenants. Both sections 137 and 138 shed light on salvation of the dead, so their addition to the scriptural canon was timely, coming in an era of unprecedented temple-building activity.

To Whom Did the Savior Preach? (Verses 18-30). President Smith's vision has shed further light on Peter's declaration that the Lord preached to those "who sometime [the Revised Standard Version says "formerly"] were disobedient." The Savior did not go "in person" to the "ungodly" or "unrepentant" (D&C 138:20, 29). Rather, President Smith learned, the Master "organized his forces," authorizing righteous spirits to carry the gospel message to those to whom he could not personally go. (See Joseph Fielding Smith, *Answers to Gospel Questions* 1:27-29.) This work continues, and faithful elders of the present dispensation can look forward to continuing their preaching of the gospel even after they have left mortality. (See verses 30 and 57.)

"The Acceptable Day of the Lord" (Verse 31). This phrase is undoubtedly related to references in the King James Bible to "the acceptable year of the Lord" (Isaiah 61:2 and Luke 4:19). Other modern versions translate this phrase as "the year of God's favor." Hence the Lord's authorized representatives are declaring to the inhabitants of the spirit world that the time has come when they are to enjoy the Lord's favor and his full acceptance on condition of their repentance.

Elias or Elijah (Verses 45-48). The "Elias" who appeared on the Mount of Transfiguration was known as "Elijah" in the Old Testament, and was the same individual Malachi prophesied would come in the latter days. (Compare Malachi 4:5-6 with Moroni's paraphrase of this prophecy in D&C section 2. See the discussion of meanings of "Elias" under section 27 herein.) President Smith emphasized that Elijah's keys, like the Savior's mission in the spirit world, were closely related to "the great work to be done in the temples" (verse 48).

Bondage in the Spirit World (Verses 50-51). Although we generally identify "spirit prison" with the condition of only the wicked, in at least one sense all spirits—both good and evil—consider their existence in the spirit world as a bondage. (See verse 50.) Hence when the Savior announced to them that they would soon be resurrected, he truly was "declaring liberty to the captives" who had eagerly been looking forward to "the hour of their deliverance from the chains of death" (verse 18).

Latter-day Leaders (Verses 53-56). At this point President Smith's vision shifted from the spirits who had already been on earth in previous eras. He now saw those who had been chosen to become leaders of the Church in the latter days.

Official Declaration 1 or "Manifesto"

Joseph Smith first received revelation concerning the principle of plural marriage during the 1830s (see the discussion of plural marriage under section 132 herein) but was not permitted to teach it at that time. It was not until 1841, after the Saints had settled in Nauvoo, that this principle was taught and practiced secretly by the Church. In 1852 the doctrine was announced publicly for the first time.

It is impossible to state exactly how many were involved in the practice of plural marriage. Reliable estimates vary from 2 to 3 percent if only married men are counted, or about 10 to 15 percent if men, women, and children are included. Church leaders enforced strict standards in connection with authorizing plural marriages. Even though there were some abuses which attracted publicity, most plural families enjoyed rich spiritual blessings and a variety of other advantages if they were willing to put forth the requisite effort to live in this system of marriage.

Congress passed the first antibigamy law in 1862, but concern over the Civil War and Reconstruction delayed enforcement. In 1882 the Edmunds Law made it a crime to marry a plural wife (new plural marriage) or to live with one (polygamist cohabitation). The decade of the 1880s was a period of very bitter anti-Mormon agitation, resulting in the passage of the Edmunds-Tucker Law in 1887 under which Church property was confiscated and many Latter-day Saints were prevented from voting and holding office. By May 1890 the Supreme Court had upheld the Constitutionality of this law,

Wilford Woodruff (Photo courtesy Harold B. Lee Library)

and members of Congress were considering even more strict measures.

In this setting the President of the Church, Wilford Woodruff, had a most difficult decision. His choice was not between obeying a law of God or a law of man, but rather between two divine precepts, because the Lord had commanded obedience to the Constitutional law of the land. (See D&C 98:5; 58:21.) President Woodruff received a revelation showing him that under existing conditions it would be best to suspend the practice of plural marrige.

Consequently, the Endowment House, an adobe structure on Temple Square which had been built as a place where sacred ordinances could be performed until the Salt Lake Temple was finished, was torn down during November of 1889 when President Woodruff learned that unauthorized marriages were being performed there. For nearly a year, charges persisted that the Church was still sanctioning polygamous marriages. To answer these attacks, President Woodruff issued the "Official Declaration" or "Manifesto" prior to the October Conference in 1890. He subsequently explained:

The Latter-day Saints should not get the idea that the Lord has forsaken His people, or that He does not reveal His mind and will; beause such an idea is not true. The Lord is with us, and has been with us from the beginning. This Church has never been led a day except by revelation. . . .

Read the life of Brigham Young and you can hardly find a revelation that he had wherein he said, "Thus saith the Lord;" but the Holy Ghost was with him; He taught by Inspiration and by revelation. . . . Joseph said "Thus saith the Lord" almost every day of his life in laying the foundation of this work. But those who followed him have not deemed it always necessary to say "Thus saith the Lord;" yet they have led the people by the power of the Holy Ghost.

I have had some revelations of late, and very important ones to me, and I will tell you what the Lord has said to me. . . .

The Lord showed me by vision and revelation exactly what would take place if we did not stop this practice. . . .

I should have let all the temples go out of our hands; I should have gone to prison myself, and let every other man go there, had not the

God of heaven commanded me to do what I did do. . . . I went before the Lord, and I wrote what the Lord told me to write. (Deseret News, November 7, 1891.)

Excerpts from this and two other related statements by President Woodruff were included as explanatory material following Official Declaration 1 in the 1981 edition of the Doctrine and Covenants. (See pages 292-93.)

It was agreed by Church leaders and non-Mormon officials that new polygamous marriages would not be allowed, but that those who had entered plural marriage before the Manifesto was issued could continue to live with these families without fear of prosecution. It was under these terms that Utah was admitted as one of the United States in 1896. In 1904, President Joseph F. Smith again upheld the principles set forth in the Official Declaration and stressed that the Church would not sanction plural marriages anywhere in the world. Since that time, a few small groups have gained notoriety by their practice of polygamy, but such persons are subject to excommunication from the Church.

Official Declaration 2

Perhaps nothing has had a greater impact on the worldwide spread of the Church than did the 1978 revelation received through President Spencer W. Kimball extending the priesthood to worthy brethren of all races. For several months the General Authorities had discussed this topic at length in their regular temple meetings. Then, on June 1, 1978, after a three-hour temple meeting, President Kimball invited his counselors and the Twelve to remain while the other General Authorities were excused. He again brought up the possibility of conferring the priesthood on worthy brethren of all races. During the two-hour discussion "there was a marvelous outpouring of unity, oneness, and agreement in the council." The President then led the group in prayer on this matter. "It was during this prayer that the revelation came," Elder Bruce R. McConkie recalled. "The Spirit of the Lord rested mightily upon us all;

we felt something akin to what happened on the day of Pentecost and at the dedication of the Kirtland Temple." (Bruce R. McConkie, "The New Revelation on Priesthood," *Priesthood* [Salt Lake City: Deseret Book Co., 1981], p. 128.)

One week later, the statement known as Official Declaration 2 was released. This is not a record of the revelation itself, but, like Official Declaration 1, is an inspired announcement that the revelation had been received. This may explain why these documents have their present status rather than being numbered sections in the Doctrine and Covenants.

The impact of this revelation was far-reaching. Faithful Black Latter-day Saints rejoiced as they received long-hoped-for ordination to the priesthood, mission calls, calls to serve in bishoprics or stake presidencies, and the eternal blessings of the temple. Within a few months, missions were opened in the predominantly Black nations of Nigeria and Ghana, and hundreds of converts were baptized.

Subsequent Revelation

It is the firm testimony and witness of the present author that later presidents of the Church have been prophets as much as was Joseph Smith and that they, too, have received divine revelation to guide the Church. (See Appendix B for a list of selected published revelations.) Some ask why these subsequent revelations have not been added to the Doctrine and Covenants canon. There are several thoughts which might be considered in relation to this question.

The idea that recorded revelations came at an even pace throughout Joseph Smith's life and then suddenly ceased with his death is erroneous. Over half of the revelations now recorded in the Doctrine and Covenants were received in the three-year period 1830–1832, and there were several years nearer the end of the Prophet's life during which no such revelations were received. (See the "Chronological Order of Contents" in the Doctrine and Covenants and the chart on p. 7 herein.) Unlike the earlier revelations in which new fundamentals were made known, later revelations were more in the nature of application of previously revealed principles.

Mormon, who abridged the Nephite history, explained that he had included less than a hundredth part of the original record, even of Christ's visit. He challenged his readers by promising that when they were able to understand and live the lesser part, then they might expect to receive the greater part. (See 3 Nephi 26:6–9.) The same principle applies to latter-day revelation. In a sense, the Lord would condemn his people by including in the formal scriptural canon precepts they were not prepared to live. (For further discussion of this subject, see Joseph Fielding Smith, *Doctrines of Salvation* 3:201–202; Bruce R. McConkie, "A New Commandment," *Ensign* [August 1976], p. 7)

Finally, those who are genuinely interested in knowing the teachings of the present prophet can hear them at general conferences and read them in several Church periodicals. Elder Spencer W. Kimball testified most impressively that remarkable revelations have continued. Quoting George Q. Cannon, Elder Kimball declared: "There has never been a single minute since 1830 when the people were left without the revealed guidance of the Lord." (*CR* October 1966, p. 26.) Serious students of the Doctrine and Covenants should also study the inspired teachings given today through the Lord's living prophet.

Appendix A

Section Numbers in Various Editions

(This chart compares the number given to each section in the 1831, 1835, 1844, 1876, and 1921 editions.)

1833	1835	1844	1876, 1921	1833	1835	1844	1876, 1921	1833	1835	1844	1876, 1921
1	1	1	1		54	54	32	60	19	19	59
			2	35	55	55	33	61	70	71	60
2	30	30	3	36	56	56	34	62	71	72	61
3	31	31	4	37	11	11	35	63	72	73	62
4	32	32	5	38	57	57	36	64	20	20	63
5	8	8	6	43	58	58	37	65	21	21	64
6	33	33	7	44:	61	61	41		24	24	65
7	34	34	8	1-54	13:	13:	42:		74	75	66
8	35	35	9		1-19a	1-19a	1-72		25	25	67
9	36	36	10	44:	13:	13:	42:73		22	22	68
10	37	37	11	55-57	19b	19b			28	28	69
11	38	38	12	47:			42:		26	26	70
			13	21-24	13:20	13:20	74-77	90	91		71
12	39	39	14	47:	13:	13:	42:	89	90		72
13	40	40	15	1-20	21-23	21-23	78-93	29	29		73
14	41	41	16	45	14	14	43	73	74		74
	42	42	17	46	62	62	44	87	88		75
15	43	43	18	48	15	15	45	91	92		76
16	44	44	19	49	16	16	46				77
24	2	2	20	50	63	63	47	75	76		78
22	46	46	21	51	64	64	48	76	77		79
23	47	47	22	52	65	65	49	77	78		80
17-21	45	45	23	53	17	17	50	79	80		81
25	9	9	24		23	23	51	86	87		82
26	48	48	25	54	66	66	52	88	89		83
27	49	49	26	55	66*	67	53	4	4		84
28	50	50	27	56	67	68	54				85
30	51	51	28	57	68	69	55	6	6		86
29	10	10	29	58	69	70	56				87
31-33	52	52	30		27	27	57	6*	7		88
34	53	53	31	59	18	18	58	80	81		89

1833	1835	1844	1876, 1921	1835	1844	1876, 1921	1835	1844	1876, 1921
	84	85	90	3	3	107		103	124
	92	93	91			108			125
	93	94	92			109			126
	82	83	93			110		105	127
	83	84	94			111		106	128
	95	96	95		104	112			129
	96	97	96			113			130
	81	82	97			114			131
	85	86	98			115			132
	78	79	99			116	100	108	133
	94	95	100			117	101	109	
	97	98	101			118	102	110	134
	5	6	102		107	119		111	135
		101	103			120			136
	98	99	104			121			
		102	105			122			
	99	100	106			123			

*In the 1835 edition two sections were numbered "vi" and two "lxvi."

Sections 137 and 138 were added in the 1981 edition.

Appendix B

Selected Published Revelations

Many revelations have been received in addition to those included in the standard works. Many of these are available only in manuscript form. Following is a list of only a few of the revelations published in recognized Church works.

Joseph Smith Period

At least 28 published revelations are not in the Doctrine and Covenants.

1835 Reynolds Cahoon to set his house in order (*HC*, 2:299)

Morley and Partridge to attend solemn assembly (*HC*, 2:302-3)

If Whitlock repents, sins to be forgotten (*HC*, 2:315)

1838 Brigham Young to provide for his family (*HC*, 3:23)

1840 Orson Hyde's mission to Palestine shown him in a dream (*HC*, 4:375-76; see also pp. 113 and 467)

1842 Twelve to edit *Times and Seasons* according to Spirit (*HC*, 4:503)

More Recent Revelations

Church leaders testify that revelations continue:

President Brigham Young, August 1852 (*JD*, 6:282 -83)

Elder Spencer W. Kimball (*CR*, October 1966, pp. 23-26)

1847 Brigham Young's vision of Joseph Smith

(*Improvement Era,* Nov. 1968, pp. 75-76.)

1853 Vision of the Salt Lake and future temples (*JD,* 1:133)

1877 Temple work for the signers of the Declaration of Independence and others (*JD,* 19:229)

1880 Wicked nations and the responsibility of the Twelve (Cowley, *Life of Wilford Woodruff,* pp. 530–31)

1882 Calls to be General Authorities (James R. Clark, *Messages of the First Presidency,* 2:348–49)

1883 Heber J. Grant's vision of council in the spirit world (*CR,* October 1942, p. 26)
Church to be guided through appointed channels (*Messages of the First Presidency,* 2:354)

1889 Message of assurance (*Messages of the First Presidency,* 3:175)

1890 The Manifesto announcing the end of plural marriages was the result of revelation (Wilford Woodruff in *Deseret News,* November 7, 1891)

1894 Trace genealogy and be sealed to ancestors (*Messages of the First Presidency,* 3:251–60)

1898 Christ personally instructed Lorenzo Snow to organize the First Presidency (LeRoi C. Snow, "An Experience of My Father's," *Improvement Era,* September 1933, p. 677)

1899 Word of the Lord on tithing (*Messages of the First Presidency* 3:312)

1935 Put the priesthood to work (*CR,* October, 1972, p. 124)

Selected Bibliography

Berrett, William E. *Teachings of the Doctrine and Covenants.* Salt Lake City: Deseret Book Company, 1956.

Bluth, John V. *Concordance to the Doctrine and Covenants.* Salt Lake City: Deseret Book Company, 1968.

Church Educational System. *The Doctrine and Covenants Student Manual.* Salt Lake City: The Church of Jesus Christ of Latter-day Saints, 1981.

Cook, Lyndon W. *The Revelations of the Prophet Joseph Smith.* Provo, Utah: Seventy's Mission Book Store, 1981.

Doxey, Roy W. *The Doctrine and Covenants and the Future.* Salt Lake City: Deseret Book Company, 1960.

———. *The Doctrine and Covenants Speaks.* Salt Lake City: Deseret Book Company, 1964.

———. *Latter-day Prophets and the Doctrine and Covenants.* Vols. 1–4. Salt Lake City: Deseret Book Company, 1963–65.

Lambert, Asael Carlyle. *The Published Editions of the Doctrine and Covenants of the Church of Jesus Christ of Latter-day Saints in All Languages, 1833 to 1950.* (no publisher, no date.)

Ludlow, Daniel H. *A Companion to Your Study of The Doctrine and Covenants.* 2 vols. Salt Lake City: Deseret Book Company, 1978.

Lyon, T. Edgar. *An Introduction to the Doctrine and Covenants and the Pearl of Great Price.* Salt Lake City: LDS Department of Education, 1948.

McGavin, E. Cecil. *The Historical Background of the Doctrine and Covenants.* Salt Lake City: Paragon Printing Company, 1949.

Otten, L. G., and C. M. Caldwell. *Sacred Truths of the Doctrine and Covenants.* 2 vols. Springville, Utah: LEMB, Inc., 1982, 1983.

Petersen, Melvin J. "A Study of the Nature of and the Significance of the Changes in the Revelations as Found in a Comparison of the Book of Commandments and Subsequent Editions of the Doctrine and Covenants." Master's thesis, Brigham Young University, 1955.

Rasmussen, Ellis T. "Textual Parallels to the Doctrine and Covenants and Book of Commandments as Found in the Bible." Master's thesis, Brigham Young University, 1951.

Smith, Hyrum M., and Sjodahl, Janne M. *Doctrine and Covenants Commentary.* Salt Lake City: Deseret Book Company, 1955.

Smith, Joseph. *History of the Church.* Vols. 1–7. Salt Lake City: *Deseret News,* 1902–12.

Smith, Joseph Fielding. *Church History and Modern Revelation.* Vols. 1–2. Salt Lake City: Council of the Twelve Apostles, 1953.

Sperry, Sidney B. *Doctrine and Covenants Compendium.* Salt Lake City: Bookcraft, 1960.

Widtsoe, John A. *The Message of the Doctrine and Covenants.* Salt Lake City: Bookcraft, 1969.

Wood, Wilford C. *Joseph Smith Begins His Work.* Vol. 2. (Includes photographic reproductions of the 1831 and 1835 editions of the Doctrine and Covenants.) Salt Lake City: Deseret News Publishing Company, 1962.

Index